Holding Hands

Devotions for Women

by Catherine Duerr

CPH
SAINT LOUIS

Scripture quotations taken from the HOLY BIBLE, NEW INTERNATIONAL VERSION®. NIV®. Copyright © 1973, 1978, 1984 by International Bible Society. Used by permission of Zondervan Publishing House. All rights reserved.

Copyright © 2000 Concordia Publishing House
3558 S. Jefferson Avenue, St. Louis, MO 63118-3968
Manufactured in the United States of America

Library of Congress Cataloging-in-Publication Data

Duerr, Catherine.
  Holding hands / Catherine Duerr.
    p. cm.
  ISBN 0-570-05243-2
  1. Christian women—Religious life. I. Title.
  BV4527 D84 2000
  242'.643—dc21   99-050850

1 2 3 4 5 6 7 8 9 10   09 08 07 06 05 04 03 02 01 00

WITH LOVE TO STEVE.
I thank God for giving you to me
to be my husband. Your love,
encouragement, and support
have been a blessing to me.

Contents

I pray that out of His glorious riches
He may strengthen you with power
through His Spirit in your inner being,
so that Christ may dwell in your hearts
through faith. And I pray that you, being rooted
and established in love, may have power,
together with all the saints, to grasp how wide
and long and high and deep is the love of Christ,
and to know this love that surpasses knowledge—
that you may be filled to the measure of all
the fullness of God. Now to Him who is able to do
immeasurably more than all we ask or imagine,
according to His power that is at work within us,
to Him be glory in the church and in Christ Jesus
throughout all generations, for ever and ever!
Amen.

Ephesians 3:16-21

Spilt Milk

My 5-year-old son, Mark, stood up and reached across the table for another meatball. As his hand traveled back over the table, his elbow caught his milk cup, knocking it over and spilling the contents on the floor.

Staring at the white puddle on my freshly mopped floor, I wanted to cry. This immediately brought to mind the old saying, "There's no use crying over spilt milk."

As I retrieved a rag to clean up the mess, my mind countered with, "It might not do any good to cry, but I just mopped the floor." With three kids, a dog, a cat, and two adults, it doesn't take long for the floor to look pretty bad. I had been busy with so many other pressing chores, it had taken me longer than usual this week to find time for mopping. So by the time I had dragged out the mop that morning, there were black spots where juice had spilled and collected dirt over several days. When I had finished, I was pleased with how good it looked until ... I just wanted to cry.

Bearing the title of "housewife," I can echo the words in Ecclesiastes and declare that everything is "meaningless." I do the same chores over and over again and wonder what I have gained.

When God turns my attention to Him, though, I see that my job description goes beyond cooking and cleaning. I am a builder—building under God's authority and direction. Although I have various side jobs, my main projects at this point are my children as I raise them and teach them about Jesus. I want to help them celebrate their gift of faith in Christ and the promises and privileges this gift brings.

The seemingly mundane tasks that I perform are the building blocks that provide a foundation on which my family can grow. Mopping floors and doing laundry are not glamorous, but they are part of the work that allows me time to share God's Word and His love with my family.

Dear God,

Sometimes I become bogged down with what seems to be meaningless tasks, and I feel as though I am getting nowhere. Give me Your perspective to see beyond the mundane and into eternity. Remind me of the awesome responsibility You have entrusted to me in my children. Guide me as I teach them to know, love, and honor You. In Jesus' name. Amen.

Therefore we do not lose heart. Though outwardly we are wasting away, yet inwardly we are being renewed day by day. For our light and momentary troubles are achieving for us an eternal glory that far outweighs them all. So we fix our eyes not on what is seen, but on what is unseen. For what is seen is temporary, but what is unseen is eternal.
2 Corinthians 4:16–18

Valuable Lesson

"Mark, did you finish straightening the magazines?" Grandma called to my son, who was in the living room.

"It's all done," he replied.

"Okay, you can get three 'monies' out of the money dish," she answered.

I smiled across the kitchen table at my mom.

"There are pennies, nickels, dimes, and quarters in that dish. Who knows how much money he will take," Mom said and laughed.

"He'll take three pennies," I answered. Mark had been doing chores for me too. I had tried to discuss with him the value of the different coins. But he felt cheated if I only gave him two quarters for a hard chore, like cleaning up after the dog. He would much rather have five pennies. In fact, he wanted pennies more than any other coin.

Mark came into the kitchen and showed Grandma his three pennies. I smothered a smile. "Mark, you could have chosen three of the big silver coins. Then we could have taken them home and Mommy would have traded those for a whole bunch of pennies," I told him.

"Can I do that, Grandma?" he asked.

"I will give you another job, and you can choose three more coins," she answered.

Mark finally listened to me and had the opportunity to see how much more the quarters were worth than the pennies.

As I counted 75 pennies into my son's cupped hands, I thought about the value of the treasures God has given me. My quest for more money and things can sometimes consume me, but possessions are like pennies. Even if I had a lot of individual things, I would not have much of value. But God has given me more than a few pennies. He has given me quarters, dimes, and nickels too.

Like Mark, I can get caught up in counting my pennies and hardly notice how richly God has blessed me. My faith is a shining silver dollar, a gift from my heavenly Father. Its value is measured in the flesh and blood my Savior sacrificed on the cross for me. My quarters are the members of my family. I would not trade those quarters for thousands of pennies, but I sometimes forget to realize their tremendous worth. One friend may be only one coin, but that coin's value is worth more than hundreds of pennies.

I still fantasize about winning a sweepstakes, but I realize now that all those pennies would not equal in value the riches that God already has given to me.

Dear Father,

I sometimes forget about the value of the treasures that You have given me. You know the true worth of Your blessings and how loved I am. Thank You for giving me so much, especially the gift of faith and the love of my family and friends. I truly am rich. In Your Son's name. Amen.

Command those who are rich in this present world not to be arrogant nor to put their hope in wealth, which is so uncertain, but to put their hope in God, who richly provides us with everything for our enjoyment. 1 Timothy 6:17

Only Frosting Deep

The aroma of fresh donuts overwhelmed me as we walked into the bakery. The boys ran to the glass case to check out the treats.

"You can each pick one donut," I said.

"I want the orange one." Mark pointed to his choice and watched as the clerk reached in and pulled out a cake donut with orange frosting.

"Me won orange wif 'prinklers," Nicholas said.

"He wants an orange one with sprinkles," I translated for the clerk.

Nicholas jumped up and down as the clerk picked up his donut. "Yeah! Yeah! That one!" he cried.

I smiled and surveyed the case. The boys had both picked a festively decorated Halloween donut. My attention was drawn to the center of the case, to one of my favorites—bavarian cream. From a 3-year-old's point of view, it was nothing spectacular. It was just a plain brown blob. Not even one 'prinkler. But the brown blob was chocolate frosting. For me, this was much more exciting than the colorful orange. Inside this pastry was the thick cream filling that really gave this donut its character.

All alone at the end of the case sat the apple fritters. If the bavarian creams are plain looking, the apple fritters are ugly, all twisted and gnarled. But tucked into all the little nooks and crannies are bits of apple and cinnamon. The tastiness of this pastry makes up for what it lacks in festive accessories.

The children did not see beyond the frosting that covered the top of the donut. I could look past the plain or ugly outer appearance to see the good stuff inside.

This is how God looks at people. While I can see how people seem to be, God sees inside to how they really are. He sees Christ living in the hearts of His children. If Christ lives in us, we may be physically plain, we may make visible mistakes, but Christ brings to us all the beauty and perfection we need. Instead of the plainness or the ugliness of our human nature, God sees the beauty of Christ's perfect sacrifice for us. We are oozing with God's wonderful stuff on the inside.

Dear Father,

Help me to look past the surface to find Your good stuff in myself and in others. In Jesus' name. Amen.

The LORD does not look at the things man looks at. Man looks at the outward appearance, but the LORD looks at the heart.
1 Samuel 16:7b

Lasting Impressions

T hey poured the cement today," my mom's voice said over the phone line. "Can you bring the boys over so we can get their handprints?"

"How soon do we need to be there?" I asked as I looked at my watch to determine how long Mark had been sleeping.

"I thought they were going to do it a little later in the day, but Dad just got back from the new house and said they are almost finished with the cement," Mom explained. "We'll need to go over pretty soon if we are going to get the handprints."

"Mark is sleeping," I said.

"Can you wake him?" she asked.

"I suppose I could," I said with a sigh. Waking up sleeping children is not my idea of a smart move, but my mom really wanted her grandchildren's handprints pressed into the porch at the house they were building.

When we arrived at the new house, Mark didn't want to have anything to do with putting his hand in that goo. We started with Nicholas. My mom held Nicholas next to the newly poured walkway while I placed his hand on the cement and gently pressed on it. He grinned.

"Okay, Mark, it's your turn," I said.

"No! I don' wanna." He turned away.

"Nick did it. It doesn't hurt," I said.

"No!"

"If you don't do it now, it will be too hard later,"
I explained.

No amount of persuading or encouraging could get
Mark to change his mind. So we used a stick to scratch
"Mark and Nick" and the date into the cement. It hardened with just the one little handprint.

Grandma and Grandpa have lived in their house for several years now, and still there is only one little handprint
in the cement. Mark missed his opportunity. The only
time he could make an impression was when the cement
was wet.

I think of my children as wet cement. Now, when they
are young, I have the opportunity to leave lasting impressions on their lives. The lessons that I teach, the values
that I instill, the love that I share now will imprint their
lives forever. I don't want to miss the opportunity to
impress on their hearts that Jesus loves them and died
and rose for them so they can live forever. I pray that
when the cement hardens, that assurance will stay with
them forever.

Dear God,

Please be with me as I raise my children. Help me
as I teach them about You, Your love, and Your salvation. In Jesus' name. Amen.

*Love the LORD your God with all your heart and
with all your soul and with all your strength.
These commandments that I give you today are to
be upon your hearts. Impress them on your children. Talk about them when you sit at home and
when you walk along the road, when you lie
down and when you get up. Deuteronomy 6:5–7*

Freedom

After receiving our permission to get out of bed to get a drink of water, Mark danced all the way down the hall. He was glad to have an excuse to get up. He had just arrived in the living room when we heard what sounded like more pitter-patter coming down the hallway. Steve and I both looked up and saw 2-year-old Nicholas enter the room with a triumphant grin on his face. Apparently he had figured out how to get out of his crib.

I carried my little boy to his bedroom and put him in the crib, saying, "It's time to go night-night, sweetie. I love you."

After I tucked him in, I had barely returned to my place on the couch when he was out in the living room, delighted with his newfound freedom.

Steve took Nicholas back and put him in the crib. I took him two more times, and Steve took him three more times.

We finally moved Mark into our bed and closed the boys' bedroom door. Nicholas was able to get out of the crib, but he could not leave the room. He cried himself to sleep right next to the door. When I went to check on him that last time, I gently picked him up and placed him in his crib.

Like Nicholas, I have been set free. Because of Christ's death and resurrection, I am freed from sin. I am no longer a prisoner and no longer bound by the Law. I am saved through faith in Jesus. This does not mean that I am free to sin. If I continue in my old ways, I will find myself trapped in my sin again, just like Nicholas found himself out of the crib but still trapped in the bedroom.

Nicholas now sleeps in a bed. He is free to get up, but he is also expected to stay there and get a good night's sleep. In a similar manner, I have been freed from my sins, but God gives me His Holy Spirit to use that freedom to love and serve others.

Dear Lord,

Thank You for giving me my freedom through faith in Jesus so I am no longer a slave to sin. Now that I am free, help me to serve You always. In my Savior's name. Amen.

You, my brothers, were called to be free.
But do not use your freedom to indulge the sinful
nature; rather, serve one another in love.
Galatians 5:13

Plastic or Porcelain?

You young ladies should use your nice dishes. So many of the young people today leave them stored away instead of using them," Eva said, sharing her opinion with the ladies at the Bible study.

"Sometimes I just take the storage containers from the refrigerator, put them in the microwave, then set them on the table," I confessed. My attitude was that no one noticed anyway and this gave me more time for reading or playing games with my children.

Eva turned, looked at me, and asked, "Don't you have a dishwasher?"

Stunned, all I could do was nod. Then I started to feel offended. I had hoped to be patted on the back for taking shortcuts so I could use my time for things of more value.

That evening, as I was preparing dinner, I looked at the leftover green beans in the plastic margarine tub I had just taken from the refrigerator. *It really wouldn't be that much trouble to dump these in a nice bowl and put the bowl in the dishwasher after dinner,* I thought. Maybe Eva had a point.

In Titus 2, God teaches that the older women should train the younger women. I used to read this as a directive to older women. Because I didn't see myself as "older" yet, it was something to store away for later reference.

But as a younger woman, that verse is for me too. God

has placed special people in my life. Their wisdom comes from years of experience not only in table setting, but also in using all of God's gifts to us, whether great or small. As a younger woman, I can take advantage of the counsel these friends offer and ask God to keep my pride from getting in the way.

Although storage containers sometimes still appear on my table, I have made a more conscious effort to set a nice table for my family, as I would for a guest. After all, we do have a Guest at every meal, a Savior, no less. Christ willingly died to pay for our sins, rose to bring us the hope of heaven, and dwells within our hearts and homes. Shouldn't we set our best tables—in fact, do our best in all we do—for the glory and honor of such a Guest?

Dear God,

Thank You for the wonderful people You have given to me as counselors. Their wisdom is truly appreciated. Remind me that they are gifts from You to train me to use Your other gifts wisely and to Your glory. In Jesus' name. Amen.

Listen to advice and accept instruction, and in the end you will be wise. Proverbs 19:20

Kindred Spirits

When I returned to work at the bank after my second miscarriage, I was ready to immerse myself in my job so I could try to put this episode behind me as quickly as possible. As I placed my lunch in the refrigerator, I heard Barb say, "We probably will have our babies about the same time."

I turned around and looked at my coworker, unsure of what to say. She was beaming. Before I could say anything, Barb added, "Oh, you weren't here when I told everyone. I'm pregnant too."

I didn't want to be rude, but I thought the best thing would be to clear up the misunderstanding right away. "I lost my baby."

"Oh, I'm sorry. No one told me."

I forced a smile as I shook my head, "It's okay." Then I tried to switch the subject back to her. "When are you due?"

I didn't know Barb very well, but I liked her. She worked at the teller station next to mine, and she seemed nice.

A couple days later, Barb wasn't at work. News about her condition filtered in throughout the day. My tension grew as she went from having a sonogram to having complications. By the end of that day, I learned that she had lost her baby too.

After work, I went shopping for a sympathy card for Barb. After looking at several, one struck a responsive chord. A wave of peace came over me as I read the words: "There is no pain on earth that heaven can't hold." I knew this was the card to give Barb.

At the time, I didn't know that Barb wasn't a Christian.

In the weeks and months that followed, Barb and I talked a lot. We talked about our loss and our pain. We talked about our desire for children. We talked about God.

Because of my hurt, God can use me to help other women who are hurting. As with Barb, I may be able to introduce someone to God. What a comfort it is to know that God understands the pain of losing a child. What a comfort it is to know that, just as the suffering and death of God's Son brought salvation to the world, God uses even my pain to do His good work.

Dear God,

Help me to use all the experiences of my life for Your glory—the good, victorious ones and the painful, hurting ones. I know that through them all, You are there, and You understand. In Your Son's name. Amen.

Praise be to the God and Father of our Lord Jesus Christ, the Father of compassion and the God of all comfort, who comforts us in all our troubles, so that we can comfort those in any trouble with the comfort we ourselves have received from God.
2 Corinthians 1:3

Ban-Aids

Nicholas stumbled into the living room and curled up on the couch. "My tummy hurts," he said.

"I know, sweetie," I said as I sat next to him and stroked his hair. "It might help if you ate a little something."

He only moaned in response.

I sighed. The doctor had given him a shot the first day he had the stomach flu so he could keep food down. It had worked, but he hadn't eaten since then. After a couple days without much food, he felt just as miserable as he had that first day. *If he isn't better by Monday, I'm taking him back to the doctor,* I thought.

"I won' a ban-aid," he whimpered.

"What for?" I asked.

"My tummy."

I was about to explain that a bandage wouldn't do a bit of good. But then I thought, *It's not going to hurt him, and if he thinks it helps, it might.*

I retrieved the box and returned to my patient. "Where does it hurt?" I asked.

"Here," he said, pointing to a spot on his stomach.

I bandaged the spot.

"And here. And here."

Five plastic adhesive strips later, I closed the box. I pulled Nicholas' shirt down over his well-bandaged abdomen and gathered him onto my lap. His spirits seemed a little better. I still felt frustrated. I wanted to be able to make him better, but there was nothing I could do ... besides pray.

It occurred to me that this is the very way I stand before God—helpless. All of my good works are like the bandages I placed on Nicholas' tummy. It looks like I am doing something, but I'm really not accomplishing anything. Only God's free gift of faith in Christ brings me salvation and relief from the pain of sin.

God alone heals bodies and souls, but with God working in me, I am anything but helpless. My prayers, though they may seem inadequate, go to an almighty and powerful God. I may be weak, but He is strong. He will hear my request and heal Nicholas in His perfect time.

Dear Father,

Sometimes I get so caught up in trying to get things done, I forget that You provide all that is needed for spiritual and physical health. Use me as Your instrument to accomplish those tasks You give me to do. In Jesus' name. Amen.

*For it is God who works in you to will
and to act according to His good purpose.
Philippians 2:13*

Another Child to Love

I sat in the recliner and talked to my swollen belly. "It shouldn't be too much longer now and I will be able to hold you in my arms." I rubbed my tummy and pressed against the bump that I thought might be a foot.

As I sat in the chair talking to my unborn child, I wondered if I would be able to love this child like I love Mark and Nicholas. Then I remembered that I had felt the same way while pregnant with Nicholas. I had been positive that I couldn't love another child like I loved my firstborn, Mark. I wasn't sure I wanted anyone to infringe on my time with Mark.

Then Nicholas was born. It didn't take him long to snuggle his way into my heart. Although I loved Nicholas completely, it didn't in any way diminish my love for Mark. And Mark benefited because he had a brother to love. The pool of love in our family grew.

Slowly my fears and doubts concerning this new baby calmed. I knew there would be plenty of love for her and she would be a welcome addition to our family. Our love for one another would increase again.

My heavenly Father has children too—so many, in fact, that only He knows the number. He loves each and every one of us totally and unconditionally. His love for another person doesn't diminish His love for me. In fact, God's merciful love overflows my capacity to hold it. His love is so great that He didn't allow my imperfections to get in the way. Instead, He offered His Son, Jesus, as a sacrifice to pay for my sins. Even now God sends His

Holy Spirit to assure me that nothing can diminish His
love for me.

Dear Father,

Your perfect love is more than I can fathom.
The reality of that love come to earth in my Savior,
Jesus Christ, overwhelms me. Help me to share
the Good News of Your saving love with others.
In my Savior's name. Amen.

*For I am convinced that neither death nor life,
neither angels nor demons, neither the present
nor the future, nor any powers, neither height nor
depth, nor anything else in all creation, will be
able to separate us from the love of God that is in
Christ Jesus our Lord. Romans 8:38–39*

Adoption

It was our last adoption class. I tried to pay attention to the lessons on the legal aspects of adoption, but I was distracted. There was a hollowness in my stomach that reminded me of when I had been pregnant. Even if I ate, I didn't seem to be able to fill that spot. I wondered if I was pregnant. But we had already started this adoption process; I didn't want another miscarriage to slow things down.

Weeks later, when the caseworker called to set up a home visit, I divulged my news. "I've had a positive pregnancy test," I stated. Before the caseworker could respond, I added, "But I haven't been successful in the past. I don't want this to delay anything."

She assured me that if something happened to the baby I was carrying, we would pick up right where we had left off. Several months later, I gave birth to a healthy, baby boy. I was smitten with Mark instantly.

We never completed the adoption process, but to this day, I know I would have loved an adopted child just as much as I love Mark, Nicholas, and Angela.

Once I asked a friend who had adopted one child and given birth to two if she loved her children differently. She said she loved them all differently because they were different people, but she loved them all equally.

This reality was important to me, not because I had wanted to adopt but because I am adopted. The Bible refers to us as God's adopted children. Despite what some people think, adoption does not carry a lesser status.

If my baby grew in my womb or in someone else's, he or she would still be very much my child. Through the waters of Baptism, I am very much God's child. I have all the rights and privileges of being His daughter: the forgiveness Jesus won for me on the cross and, through Jesus' resurrection, the promise of an eternal inheritance in heaven.

Dear Father,

I rejoice that I am fully Your child. Thank You for sealing my adoption in the waters of Baptism and for making me a member of Your family. In Jesus' name. Amen.

The Spirit Himself testifies with our spirit that we are God's children. Now if we are children, then we are heirs—heirs of God and co-heirs with Christ, if indeed we share in His sufferings in order that we may also share in His glory.
Romans 8:16–17

The Inside Line

I held the envelope in my hand, not daring to look at it or even to feel it too much. This was the editor's response to the latest story I had submitted to the magazine. I had high hopes for this one. Less than a month before I had attended a conference and sat face to face with the editor. We had discussed what he wanted. I had taken careful notes and tailored my story to meet all of his specifications. I felt confident because I had the inside line.

Still not really looking at the envelope, I tore a corner and slid my finger across the top. The *P.S.* caught my eye first and told me everything I needed to know. It read, "Nice try!" I forced myself to read the letter as the editor explained that my story was terrific, but they just didn't have the space.

Later, when I reread the letter, I noticed the words that I believe God wanted me to see. "May the Lord guide you ..." I thought about those words. Had the Lord guided me? I knew I had taken control because I thought I had the inside line. I thought I knew exactly what the editor wanted. I had written for the editor rather than for God.

In the business world, it is important to know what the market wants and to provide it. But my writing is not a business, it is a God-given vocation. He has provided me with a talent and the opportunity to use that talent to praise Him. He also promises to guide my efforts.

Whether my vocation is writing, caring for my family, or teaching Sunday school, God will work through me.

When He works through me, there is no limit to what can be accomplished. With God, I do have the inside line.

Dear Lord,

Guide me in the ways You want me to go. Send Your Holy Spirit to help me follow You. Use me to bring honor and glory to Your name and to tell others of Your Son, my Savior. In His name. Amen.

If anyone speaks, he should do it as one speaking the very words of God. If anyone serves, he should do it with the strength God provides, so that in all things God may be praised through Jesus Christ. To Him be the glory and the power for ever and ever. Amen. 1 Peter 4:11

What Do I Deserve?

I caught Mark by the arm and drew him toward me. As he crawled into my lap, I said, "You were so good at Uncle Don's birthday party last night."

He grinned and said, "I know."

I smiled.

"What do I get?" he asked.

"What do you get?" I repeated as the smile left my face.

"Because I was good."

As I searched for the right thing to say, my mind drifted to the night before. Both Mark and Nicholas had made me proud. They had minded their manners, shown respect for others, and enjoyed themselves. I had been pleased because they had been well-behaved, well-mannered boys.

I took a deep breath and explained to Mark that though there had been times when I had given him special treats for exceptional achievements, his father and I would provide for all that he needed without requiring him to earn anything. In fact, he shouldn't ask for or anticipate a reward for doing what was expected, like obeying us or treating others with respect.

As I thought about this discussion with Mark, I realized that I also think I deserve something special. I try to do what I think God expects of me, but then I expect a reward for my obedience. I easily fall into the false belief that I am good enough on my own and that God owes me something for doing the right thing.

But Isaiah tells us the reality about the "good things" we do. They are like dirty rags (Isaiah 64:6). And Jesus points out that even if we appear to obey God in most things, we can never keep the Law perfectly, which is what God demands (Matthew 5:48, James 2:10). And failing to obey God's Law perfectly results in eternal death (Romans 6:23).

Only Jesus kept the Law perfectly. He lived this perfect life in our place and took all our sins to the cross and left them there. Because of Jesus' death, we have the gift of forgiveness for the times we do not obey God's Law. Through the waters of Baptism, we have been given a new life, one in which the Holy Spirit is at work to help us do those things God expects of us.

Dear Father,

Remind me that You love me and that through
the death and resurrection of Your Son, Jesus,
You give me what I could never earn—forgiveness
and eternal life with You. In Jesus' name. Amen.

*Now to Him who is able to do immeasurably
more than all we ask or imagine, according to
His power that is at work within us, to Him
be glory in the church and in Christ Jesus
throughout all generations, for ever and ever!
Amen. Ephesians 3:20–21*

A Glimpse of Eternity

My friend Berna was given a rare gift. She faced death and, in the process, caught a glimpse of eternity.

She didn't see a light or anything like that. Instead, her kidneys started to fail. As her condition worsened, she had to face many tough choices. The tears flowed as she considered dialysis.

"I feel like I am trapping my family," she shared with me. "If I'm 'tied' to a dialysis machine, we can't travel. I can't do the things with Keith that I want to do. I might not even live to see him grow up. Tom can't change jobs because the insurance would probably not pay for dialysis because it would be a preexisting condition."

Finally, Berna reached the point where something had to be done or she would die. Her biggest struggle was thinking about leaving her husband and 3-year-old son. God brought her to the realization that He would take care of her family, even if she wasn't there. Through the power of the Holy Spirit, Berna placed the entire situation—her life and her family—into God's hands. She trusted Him to take care of her and her family. God provided her with peace as she relaxed in the knowledge that the same God who had kept His promise to send a Savior to win her forgiveness and salvation on the cross was still caring for her and her family today.

Berna's brother and sister each lovingly offered her a kidney. Not long after, she received a new kidney from her brother.

When Berna came home from the hospital, she came home with a new kidney and a new perspective on life. "All this rushing around that people do and the little things that seem to weigh on people's minds seem so insignificant," she told me. "What difference does it make in the long run of eternity? If you have faith in God, nothing else matters."

I'm one of those people that Berna sees rushing around, allowing little things to weigh on my mind. What difference will all these little things make when it comes to eternity? What really matters in my life?

Dear Lord,

Remind me daily what is truly important, what will last forever. Place my focus on these eternal things, strengthening my faith through the power of Your Holy Spirit working through Word and Sacrament. Keep me from becoming lost in the superficial things that will only pass away. In Jesus' name. Amen.

My days are like the evening shadow; I wither away like grass. But You, O LORD, sit enthroned forever; Your renown endures through all generations. Psalm 102:11–12

Whatever It Takes

A red and blue striped shirt, suspenders, baseball cap, and beard. He looked nothing like a doctor. But as unconventional as he looked, he seemed knowledgeable in his field. He shared common-sense ideas with the moms who had gathered to hear him speak.

Suddenly, I was not listening anymore. I had been brought up short by an illustration and had not moved on with the rest of the room to the next topic. The doctor had said, "If your child was in the street and about to be hit by a car, you would do whatever it took to get him to safety, even if you had to break his arm."

In my mind, I could see 18-month-old Mark in the middle of the street. A '57 Chevy was barreling toward him. I ran out and grabbed him by the arm. The car was coming fast, so I yanked on him. We narrowly escaped, but Mark fell to the ground, breaking his arm.

It pained me to think about hurting him. But the alternative … I could not even think about that.

God took a drastic step to save me. He sent His only Son to suffer and die for my sins. As His beloved child, God will not let me stand in the path of destruction. He will not let me be plowed over without saving me. A broken arm, a broken leg, a broken spirit is minor compared to the alternative.

Because I love my son, it is difficult to consider doing anything that might cause him pain, even if it is for his good. I know God's great love for me forced Him to do something that must have been painful—sacrifice His only Son. But just as I will do what it takes to save my precious child from certain doom, God did what it takes to save me because He loves me and wants me to be with Him in heaven forever.

Dear Father,

I know You love me and have done what was necessary to save me from my sins. Help me to cling to the faith in Jesus, my Savior, that You have given me, even when things are difficult. Keep me from all harm and danger. In Jesus' name. Amen.

*[God] wants all men to be saved and to come to
a knowledge of the truth. 1 Timothy 2:4*

Broken Irises

Mark followed his father around the yard, helping with the gardening. "Who's been breaking our flowers?" Steve asked. Where there had once been nine blue irises, there were now only seven.

Mark looked at the broken stalks and said, "Oh, someone broke our flowers. Who did it, Daddy?"

"I don't know," Steve responded as he cut back the broken stalks.

I picked up one of the broken flowers. "I'll put this in a vase and we can enjoy it for a little longer."

"Make them stop breaking our flowers," Mark said.

I smiled. "I can't unless I know who did it."

The neighborhood children like to play in our yard even when our boys are not outside. My best guess was that one of the children had collided with our flowers while playing.

As I looked for a vase, I considered that even knowing who had destroyed the flowers wouldn't necessarily mean we could prevent a similar incident. Our influence with the neighborhood children is not as great as it is with our own. We could talk to them, but if they didn't listen, we couldn't do much more to change their behavior. There is no practical way to guard irises against vandalism.

God's Law, the Ten Commandments, is similar to a discussion with neighborhood children about backyard etiquette. God talked to us about His expectations and gave us His commandments to guide our behavior. But on our own, we can't obey a single command. His Law is powerless to change our sinful behavior. The promised benefit of mercy (Exodus 20:5) that God extends to those who keep His commands serves as yet another reminder that we can't follow His will perfectly.

But God has a solution for our inability to keep His Law. He sent someone who could keep it perfectly in our place. Jesus faced all the temptations we face and kept each of God's commands. He took with Him to the cross the countless times we fail to obey God's Law. Because of Jesus' death, we have forgiveness for all our sins. Because of His resurrection, we have the promise of a heavenly mansion. Because of the gift of the Holy Spirit through Word and Sacrament, we have the power and privilege to live a new life according to God's commands.

Dear God,

Forgive me for Jesus' sake for the many times I break Your Law. Strengthen me through daily interaction with Your Word and through participation in Your Holy Meal as I walk in this life. Send Your Holy Spirit to guide me in Your ways. In my Savior's name. Amen.

This is love for God: to obey His commands. And His commands are not burdensome, for everyone born of God overcomes the world. This is the victory that has overcome the world, even our faith. Who is it that overcomes the world? Only he who believes that Jesus is the Son of God. 1 John 5:3–5

So Happy

When we get home, can I see if Abraham can play?" Mark asked from the backseat of the car.

"We are going to have dinner as soon as we get home," I answered.

"After dinner, can I go get him?"

"I don't know, Mark."

"Pleeeease. I would really like to play with him."

"We'll see." I had made tentative plans, but I was not ready to tell Mark what they were, in case something fell through.

"It would really make me so happy if I could play with Abraham," he replied.

I smiled. I knew it would make him "so happy."

I have told God many times what would make me "so happy." I even have tried to convince Him that something was in my best interest. But God, in His wisdom, does not always give me that one thing I believe will make my life complete. Instead, He may give me something better, something I may not have considered.

After dinner, I told Mark and Nicholas to get their swimming suits on. "We are going to Mrs. Ramming's to swim," I announced.

"Yea!" Both boys started dancing on their way to their bedroom. I followed them down the hall and gently pulled Mark aside. "We could stay home so you could play with Abraham, if you like."

"No, I want to swim!" he assured me.

God invites me to tell Him the desires of my heart, but He also asks me to trust Him to know what is best. Jesus' disciples would have been "so happy" if Jesus had escaped from the arresting mob in Gethsemane. Some of Jesus' followers would have been "so happy" if Jesus had defeated the Roman army and reestablished the Jewish nation. Instead, what a greater gift God gave to us because Jesus followed God's plan for the salvation of the world all the way to the cross—and the empty tomb.

God sees a broader picture than I do, and He will surprise and delight me with more than I could imagine.

Dear Father,

You know what I need. Remind me that You only want to give me what is best. Point me again and again to the solution for sins that You provided in Jesus, Your Son. It wasn't what humans might have expected, but it was the perfect way to restore me as Your child. Send Your Holy Spirit to guide my actions and prayers into the paths You would have me choose. In Jesus' name. Amen.

Delight yourself in the LORD and He will give you the desires of your heart. Psalm 37:4

A Tall One

S he's tall," Steve said and nodded his head toward the right as we strolled hand in hand through the busy shopping plaza.

I looked in the direction he had indicated and saw an attractive woman who was about six feet tall. "She's pretty," I agreed. After years together, I have come to understand my husband's appreciation of tall women.

On the other hand, I have always felt that my height was an affliction. My legs are so long that I have a terrible time finding pants that fit. When I was in high school, I worried that I would be taller than all the boys. I always thought the petite girls were the lucky ones.

How ironic that the feature I didn't like was likely the feature that first caught Steve's attention. What I had always viewed as a curse was actually a blessing.

When God made me, He knew who I would become. He had a path laid out for me and knew what I would need along the way. He knew a tall wife would be pleasing to Steve. God had blessed me with height, even though it took me a while to see it that way.

God continues to bless me in ways that may not be readily apparent to me. Each day I ask God to help me understand how what might now seem to be a disagreeable circumstance may indeed be a blessing from Him. When I think about the eternal good that is mine because of the death of God's Son, it becomes easier to trust that God is at work in all things for my good.

Dear God,

Thank You for all Your blessings, especially the blessing of faith in Jesus, my Savior. Make me aware of those blessings I haven't yet identified. Send Your Holy Spirit to help me share my blessings and the Good News of Jesus with others. In my Savior's name. Amen.

Be joyful always; pray continually;
give thanks in all circumstances,
for this is God's will for you in Christ Jesus.
1 Thessalonians 5:16–18

Getting Ready

When Steve walked through the door, he surveyed the room, looking at all the bare windows. "What are you doing?" he asked.

"All the window coverings were filthy," I answered from the recliner where I had my feet propped up. "I took everything down, threw the curtains and valances in the washing machine, and put the window blinds in the bathtub."

I rubbed my belly as I felt the baby kick. "The living room blinds were too big for the tub, so I guess we'll have to spray them with the hose. Could you do that for me, please?" I asked.

"Sure." Steve smiled. "The way you've been nesting, that baby should come anytime."

I *was* nesting. My bags were packed, extra meals were in the freezer, and I was busy cleaning something different every day. I wanted the house to be ready for my new arrival.

Although I anticipated that the baby would come early, the days kept passing. Readiness became a constant state of activity. However, despite my preparations, when the time finally came, it actually took me by surprise. Although I had begun to feel as if this pregnancy would last forever, I was always mindful of the fact that I would one day bring a baby home.

This reminds me of Jesus' call to prepare for His return. I am to continue to live my life, but I should always expect that Jesus will arrive at the next moment. I don't know when He is coming, but I am to be ready when He does arrive. In one sense, Jesus invites us to be nesting, to be preparing ourselves and those around us for entry into our heavenly home.

God wants all people to be saved, to come to the knowledge of Jesus as their Savior. One way people know about Jesus is through proclamation of the Gospel message. If I wait to share the Good News of God's saving love in Jesus with someone, I may wait too long and not have that opportunity. Now is the time to tell others that Jesus came to this earth to save us from our sins. Now is the time to tell others that He will come again to take all believers to live with Him in heaven.

Dear God,

As I live my life, make me aware that I am only on this earth for a short time. Send Your Holy Spirit to help me make the most of my time here to share the Good News with those around me. Prepare me for my eternal future with You. Thank You for the gift of salvation that is mine because of Jesus and for the heavenly home He is busy preparing for me. In Jesus' name. Amen.

No one knows about that day or hour, not even the angels in heaven, nor the Son, but only the Father. Be on guard! Be alert! You do not know when that time will come. Mark 13:32–33

A True Helper

That tan shirt doesn't go with those gray pants," I said to my husband as I looked up from searching for my other pearl earring.

Steve stopped buttoning his shirt halfway down, looked in the mirror, and asked, "Why not?"

"Browns and grays don't go together," I answered as I held up the missing earring.

"This isn't brown, it's tan." He started unbuttoning.

"Tans and grays don't go together," I amended. I went to the living room to collect my things before we left the house.

Steve soon followed, wearing a white shirt with pastel stripes. Draped around his neck was a muted red tie.

"Steven," I said, "that tie clashes with the pink in the shirt."

Without even looking at the colors, he gave one end of the tie a yank, pulling it from around his neck.

I had made suggestions about clothing combinations to Steve before, but I was getting the impression that my advice was irritating him. I decided to keep my mouth closed and let him mix browns and blues or wear clashing reds.

When God created woman, He designed her to be the man's helper. He didn't give her the job of fixing her husband. Proverbs 14:1 says, "The wise woman builds her house, but with her own hands the foolish one tears hers down." By telling Steve that he didn't look good, I was tearing him down. I may have thought I was helping, but

I wasn't building Steve up. It probably would have been better to say, "Those pants look nice on you. And that striped shirt you just bought would be the perfect match."

Paul reminded the Christians in Ephesus that the new life we have been given by God means we are to put away our former lives (Ephesians 4:20–23). We have been called to imitate Christ, and we have the Holy Spirit to help us show kindness, compassion, love, and forgiveness to those around us (Ephesians 4:32–5:1). When we live as God's children, we focus on identifying the gifts God has given to each of us and we build one another up. In this way, the body of Christ grows and becomes strong. We help one another; we compliment and complement one another.

The funny thing is, once I stopped criticizing Steve about his clothing combinations, he began to ask for my advice.

Dear Lord,

Sometimes I forget that You ask me to build up those around me. I assume I'm doing that, but I am really tearing them down. Forgive me for Jesus' sake. Show me new ways to strengthen my relationships with those around me. Show me a new appreciation for the gifts You give to each of us. Help me to imitate Christ in all that I say and do. In His name. Amen.

Do not let any unwholesome talk come out of your mouths, but only what is helpful for building others up according to their needs, that it may benefit those who listen. Ephesians 4:29

Dream Home

A shiver ran through me as I sat in the small office. I clutched Steve's hand for reassurance. We sat side by side in cold metal chairs, looking across the desk at the young man who held our future in his hands. Actually, all he held in his hands was a credit report, but this would help determine whether we would get our dream house.

"Hmmm," the loan officer said. "It says that you were late paying this credit card bill."

I squirmed a little in my seat, trying not to be noticed. Steve started to explain about some hard decisions we had made several years ago when he was in graduate school.

I wasn't sure we could get a loan, but with interest rates so low, we felt it was worth a try.

"It says here that you have a delinquent amount on this account," the man said.

As Steve detailed the misunderstanding that we had experienced with that creditor and how it had taken a while to get things straightened out, I wondered what was on that credit report. I wouldn't have been surprised if this loan officer knew that I told a lie in first grade or that I wrote my name on the lamp table when I was 7 years old. His computer seemed capable of accessing all of my sins.

With all of my monetary sins laid bare, I thought about God and all He knows about me. I can't hide anything from God. Yet when I stand before Him at the end of time desiring a home in heaven, I won't have any problems. I will qualify for a more magnificent home than I can imagine and in a pretty good neighborhood too. It doesn't matter how bad my credit rating is, Jesus already paid the price for all my sins when He died on the cross. My credit report has been washed clean in His blood. God doesn't see my history of sin. He sees Jesus' spotless record and stamps my life "approved."

Dear God,

Thank You for sending Jesus to win forgiveness for my sins on the cross. Because of His suffering, death, and resurrection, I will live with You in paradise. In my Savior's name I pray. Amen.

For I will forgive their wickedness
and will remember their sins no more.
Hebrews 8:12

A New House

When we still lived in an apartment, I kept hoping and wishing for a house with a backyard for the children. One day, I noticed an "open house" down the street, so I went to check it out. It was a cross between a house and an apartment. It had a small backyard, which was bigger than what we had.

I came home, went to my room, and threw myself on the bed. "God," I prayed, "I sure would like to have a backyard for the boys. They need a place to play. If You could provide a way for us to rent that house down the street, it would be really nice."

We did not find a way to rent that house. Instead, we waited a little longer, and God pointed us to a nicer house with a substantial backyard. In fact, our mortgage payment was considerably less than the rent would have been on the first house. Now, when I drive by the home I prayed for so fervently, I smile. God knew exactly what we needed, and He took care of us.

As I raise my children and care for my husband, I have definite ideas about what is best and I go after it. But I know that when I construct my own solutions, I may miss the path God would have me and my family follow. For those times I put my goals above God's, I seek His forgiveness for Jesus' sake. In some ways, when I seek solutions I'm like Jesus' disciples. They wanted to send the people back to the town to buy food. However, Jesus knew that five loaves of bread and two fish would feed the thousands who were present to hear Him teach.

Because I trust God for His perfect solutions in His perfect time, I continue to work for the best for my family, constantly praying for God's guidance to build our home according to His plan.

Dear Lord,

Take my family and build us up the way You see best. Guide me as I work for You in this family, following Your directions, trusting Your wisdom, rejoicing in Your forgiveness, and sharing my faith with those around me. In Jesus' name. Amen.

Unless the LORD builds the house,
its builders labor in vain.
Psalm 127:1a

Frozen Food Fool

I slid the pans of lasagna into the freezer and surveyed the sight. I smiled as I looked at the freezer full of aluminum pans covered with foil. *Let's see,* I thought, *we can get three meals out of each big pan and one meal from the little ones.* With only a few weeks left until the baby arrived, it felt good to be getting everything in order.

I retired to the recliner and put my feet up. I was exhausted, but I felt good about my accomplishments. Steve had taken the boys to his parents for a few days, and in that time, I had made enough dinners for three weeks. Because of the advance planning, we would have easy meals to fall back on after the baby arrived and Steve returned to work.

About a month later, Steve came home from the pediatrician's office with 1-day-old Angela. Conveying the orders to me, he said, "The doctor said, 'Mom should avoid dairy products if she is nursing.' "

I thought about the three weeks' worth of food in the freezer—the food that I wouldn't let anyone eat until after the baby was born. I remembered the lasagna and casseroles covered with cheese.

I had put a lot of stock in those frozen meals, figuring that those meals would help me through the first few weeks with the new baby. I had been tempted several times during those last days of pregnancy to throw a lasagna in the oven for dinner. But instead I stood on swollen feet, fixing something so I would have the dinners when I really needed them.

Like the rich fool in the Bible, I had stored up things and counted on them to provide for me. I felt good about myself and about the fact I would be able to rely on the riches I had stored in my freezer. And like the rich fool, God showed me that I can plan and provide for my future and still not know what will happen. I can't put my faith in my own riches, but I can count on God.

God provided for my physical needs in those first few weeks after Angela was born. We had everything from chicken to ham because of the kindness of family and friends. We really didn't do any cooking for quite a while, not due to my planning, but to God's provision.

In the same way, God has taken care of all my spiritual needs. Through His Son, He has provided the salvation I could not plan for or earn. Through His Word and His Holy Meal, I am strengthened to face the many trials of this world. And among His children I have found the fellowship and support of brothers and sisters.

Dear Father,

I know You want me to be a good steward of the gifts You give to me. You want me to use my time and resources wisely. Thank You for showing me that while my human plans are not reliable, You have supplied all my needs. Thank You. In Jesus' name. Amen.

Then Jesus said to His disciples: "Therefore I tell you, do not worry about your life, what you will eat; or about your body, what you will wear. Life is more than food, and the body more than clothes. Consider the ravens: They do not sow or reap, they have no storeroom or barn; yet God feeds them. And how much more valuable you are than birds!" Luke 12:22–24

Don't Forget

Steve loaded the boys into the car as I carried out my supplies for Sunday school. I deposited the books and papers in the car and remembered I needed some ribbon for the lesson too. I found my box of craft materials stored in the garage and started rummaging through for just the right thing. Steve had finished buckling the boys into their car seats and was now in the driver's seat. As I tried to untangle a long strand of ribbon, I glanced at Steve. He was sitting there, waiting.

"Are you going to get Angela?" I called to him.

"Oh," he glanced back at her seat. "You didn't already put her in here?"

I smiled and shook my head as he got out of the car to get her.

This is one of my big fears: *Because I am running late, Mark will be late for preschool. After struggling with Mark and Nicholas to get them ready, I load the boys into the car. I snap Nicholas in his seat, and he throws a fit because he wanted to buckle himself in. Mark forgets his share toy, so I run back inside and dig through his toys to find his eagle. On the way outside, I grab the diaper bag, my Bible, and the sweet rolls for the Bible study. Once everything is situated in the car, I check my watch and discover that preschool already has started. When I arrive at preschool and move to get Angela out of the car, I realize she is still in her crib.*

This has never happened and probably never will. But I am always afraid that the boys could distract me and make me so frazzled that I leave a sleeping Angela behind.

I have three children and at times feel disoriented and out of control. God has countless children, yet He always knows exactly where I am and what I need. A war in the Middle East, a hijacking in Europe, an earthquake in Hong Kong, and a fire in the next block cannot distract God from caring for me. I do not have to worry about God forgetting me, even if I am asleep.

Dear Father,

Thank You for loving me and always being there for me. Thank You for not forgetting my need for a Savior and for sending Jesus at the right time to suffer and die to win me forgiveness and to rise again to win me eternal life. What comfort I have because I know You will never forget me or leave me behind. In Jesus' name. Amen.

Can a mother forget the baby at her breast and
have no compassion on the child she has borne?
Though she may forget, I will not forget you!
Isaiah 49:15

Through the Struggle

After walking the floor, shifting positions, and patting her back, my dad handed a crying, fussy Angela to me. I cradled her as I rocked gently back and forth while patting her bottom. She settled into my arms and quit struggling. I suppressed a smile, and my dad pretended not to notice.

Many times in the last few months, I had walked with Angela like my dad had done. I had alternated between walking, rocking, bouncing, and swaying. I had sung and talked to her. Some nights I thought I would never get to sleep. But through it all, Angela and I developed a relationship. I learned what she liked and what soothed her, like patting her bottom. She learned to know me and to trust me and to count on me, even in the rough times.

God is with me through the struggles too. God knows what will comfort me. He helps me to rely on Him and to trust Him to help me through the rough times. As I read my Bible, listen to His Word during worship, and experience His grace through His Supper, I learn who He is and He strengthens my faith in Him. Then when I face something difficult, I can nestle into His arms and feel safe, even if everything else is painful.

Dear Father,

Thank You for sending Jesus to face the roughest battle—the one with Satan—in my place. Because Jesus defeated Satan for me, I can call You *Father*. You have promised to be with me. Help me to rest in this promise. Strengthen my trust in You. In my Savior's name. Amen.

The LORD is my shepherd, I shall not be in want.
He makes me lie down in green pastures,
He leads me beside quiet waters,
He restores my soul. He guides me in paths
of righteousness for His name's sake.
Even though I walk through the valley
of the shadow of death, I will fear no evil,
for You are with me; Your rod and Your staff,
they comfort me. You prepare a table
before me in the presence of my enemies.
You anoint my head with oil; my cup overflows.
Surely goodness and love will follow me
all the days of my life, and I will dwell
in the house of the LORD forever.
Psalm 23

The Judge

I was cutting carrots in the kitchen when I heard a few muffled grunts, followed by a scream and some loud thumping. I didn't need to find out what was going on. The noisemakers came to me.

"Nick took my bear!" Mark wailed, trying to grab the bear from Nicholas.

"I thought that was Nick's bear," I said.

"I was playing with it," Mark replied.

"Nicholas, was Mark playing with that bear?"

"I won' it," Nicholas whined.

"But was Mark playing with it?"

"No." Nicholas started to walk away with the bear.

"Yes, I was," Mark said, pushing Nicholas and grabbing the bear.

"Give me the bear," I said. "I'll cut him in half and you can each have a piece." I was only joking, but I flashed the paring knife I was holding.

"Yea!" Mark cheered.

"Can I have the head?" Nicholas asked.

I turned back to my carrots and shook my head. *It had worked for Solomon,* I thought. *Why didn't it work for me?*

As I reflected on this incident, I realized that being a parent is similar to Solomon's job as king, just on a smaller scale. Each day I settle disputes, administer punishments, pass judgments, and hand down edicts. The wisdom I use to make decisions in these matters is just as vital to my children as Solomon's wisdom was to his subjects. But I cannot develop this wisdom on my own.

Sometimes I get so caught up in my duties that I forget help is available. Just as Solomon realized the magnitude of the responsibilities he faced and asked God for wisdom, I can do the same thing. The Bible says that if I ask God for wisdom, He will give it to me. Even as I ask for wisdom, I know there will be times I will fail to make the right choices. What comfort it is to know that I have access to God's forgiveness—all I have to do is ask in my Savior's name. More important, I have the privilege of sharing this forgiveness with my children and my husband.

Dear Father,

Be with me as I raise the children You have given to me. So often I feel overwhelmed by the responsibility. Give me wisdom to deal with each situation. Forgive me for the mistakes I make. Send Your Holy Spirit to strengthen my trust in You and to guide me on the paths You would have me follow. In Jesus' name. Amen.

If any of you lacks wisdom, he should ask God, who gives generously to all without finding fault, and it will be given to him. James 1:5

Nichole

Mark noticed her right away. It took me the first two weeks of preschool to figure out which little girl was Nichole.

One morning as we were getting out of the car on our way to preschool, I saw Nichole and her mother getting out of the car next to ours. "There's your friend Nichole," I said to Mark as he climbed out of the car. I was new to this preschool stuff, but I expected him to say hello, wave, or something. Instead, Mark stood beside me and watched Nichole.

I watched too. Her brown eyes matched her long, wavy hair, and the bow that kept her hair pulled out of her cherubic face coordinated with her dress. Her pink backpack bobbed up and down as she bounced by without even a glance in our direction. I looked at Mark and a new realization of what this girl meant to him worked its way into my stomach. I had to admit she was really cute, but I didn't know that 4-year-olds could have crushes.

Throughout the year, Mark continued to admire Nichole from afar. Finally, when he turned 5 years old, he invited her to his party. I was pleased because I took it as a sign of his growing self-confidence.

At the party, I scanned the children to see whose turn it was to take a swing at the piñata. As I was about to call Nichole up for her turn, I noticed that she and Mark were holding hands. *They* both seemed quite comfortable. But the look I shot at Steve screamed *I'm not ready for this!*

Mark's first girlfriend took me by surprise, but I know there will be more. I pray he will find someone to marry eventually. I sometimes wonder what Mark's future wife is doing right now. She could be learning to read, singing "Jesus Loves Me," or even getting her diaper changed.

Someday, this woman will have a tremendous effect on our lives. She will capture my son's heart, share his dreams and sorrows, and help him through crises big and small. She will be my daughter, and my grandchildren will call her *Mommy.*

Although I don't know her now, God does. I can pray for her—for the little girl she is and the woman she will become. I can pray that God will bless this very special person.

Dear Father,

Please be with the future spouses of my children. Keep them in Your tender care. Give them what they need and delight them with Your merciful love and compassion. Help them grow to be Godly men and women. If they are not part of a Christian family, send special people into their lives to witness to saving faith in Jesus Christ. In His name. Amen.

A wife of noble character who can find? She is worth far more than rubies. Her husband has full confidence in her and lacks nothing of value. She brings him good, not harm, all the days of her life. ... Charm is deceptive, and beauty is fleeting; but a woman who fears the LORD is to be praised.
Proverbs 31:10–12, 30

Bad News

I picked up the phone on the first ring because I was standing right next to it. My mother's breathless voice came over the line. "Your brother was in an accident. He is trapped in the car. 911 has already been called. We're on our way. Pray."

As soon as I hung up the phone, I literally dropped to my knees and begged God to keep Donny safe. Many anxious minutes went by until my mom called again. She said that Donny was conscious and the ambulance was taking him to the hospital. Steve and I dropped our children off at a friend's house and went to the hospital.

Within 24 hours, my mother was standing outside Donny's room, tears streaming down her face. She choked on her words. "His hip is crushed so badly that the doctors here can't fix it. He has to go to Los Angeles."

The fact that my brother was hurt so severely seemed at first to be devastating news that carried no promise of a positive resolution. Then we met the specialist who would operate on Donny. He was one of four surgeons in the world that could perform the procedure Donny needed. Even when things appeared bleakest, there was a blessing—my brother had access to one of the best doctors in the world.

When I come face-to-face with a crisis, often all I can see are the negatives. But no matter what the world dishes out, God is there, turning what was meant for destruction into good. Hate and envy drove Joseph's brothers to sell him into slavery. But God used this incident to bring

Joseph to a position of power in Egypt. Because of his authority, Joseph eventually saved his family from starvation.

Although the negative of Donny's accident brought us into contact with an excellent surgeon, I'm still not sure what positive came from the accident itself. Maybe the "good" has not yet become apparent to me. Maybe I'll never see it. But I can take comfort in the remembrance of a dark Friday that ended in an Easter sunrise and trust that my heavenly Father is at work in all situations to accomplish good for His children.

Dear God,

You can do all things. When I come across something that seems devastating, remind me of my Easter joy. Send me an extra measure of Your Holy Spirit to help me face the negatives and celebrate the positives. In my risen Savior's name. Amen.

*And we know that in all things God works
for the good of those who love Him,
who have been called according to His purpose.
Romans 8:28*

The Eyes of the Father

I rocked 4-month-old Angela as Steve rough-housed with the boys on the other side of the room. I rocked and rocked and rocked. I held Angela as she quit struggling, then relaxed her body and let her head sink into the crook of my arm. Finally her eyes grew heavy and closed. *Peace at last,* I thought.

Just as her top lashes met the bottom ones, the wrestling match on the other side of the room escalated. Mark and Nicholas had dog-piled onto Daddy, and he retaliated with tickling. As soon as she heard the squeals, Angela's eyes flew open. She looked at me and relaxed. I talked softly, "Those are just brothers. They sure do make a lot of noise, don't they?"

She did not understand the words, but my presence seemed to soothe her. Her eyes closed, and she drifted back to sleep, even amid more noise.

As I continued to rock Angela, I thought of my own life. God has promised to give peace that passes all under-standing. I can rest in this promise because of His saving love for me. Although my life may seem to be chaotic at times and I may even panic, God's gift of peace is mine because of the faith in His Son that He has worked in my heart. Just as Angela was reassured when she opened her eyes and saw me looking at her, I, too, can look into the eyes of my Father as I look into His Words and cele-brate His Holy Meal.

Once I look into my Father's eyes, I know there is noth-ing that He cannot handle. Because His love for me is greater than anything I have experienced—great enough to send His only Son to the cross for me—I rest assured that He can and will take care of me. I am able to snuggle into His arms. I can be at peace, even amid the noise.

Dear Father,

When I feel stressed, remind me that You are with me and that You have promised to give me peace. In my Savior's name I pray. Amen.

My eyes are ever on the LORD, for only He will release my feet from the snare.
Psalm 25:15

What a Good Mom

What a good mom," my friend Jean said as I
brought out the cupcakes, "to have a party
when it isn't even anyone's birthday."

I looked around the back porch at three tables
full of kids. All the children seemed to be enjoying their tea party as they buttered crackers, poured
"tea," and passed bowls of strawberries. Jean's son, Joe,
was even licking the butter off his plastic knife. The
"unbirthday" party seemed to be a success. I smiled at
Jean to acknowledge the compliment, but I knew this
wasn't what made me a "good" mom.

Although I try to be a good mom, which might include
throwing parties, it is things like staying up all night with
a sick child, getting three kids (and myself!) ready for
church and Sunday school each week, reading a story for
the 536th time, and insisting the peas be eaten before the
ice cream that are more definitive of a good mom. The
times I receive praise, such as when I throw a party, and
the times that truly define what kind of mom I am are
not always the same.

I think the same holds true with God. I have heard more
than one Christian say, "Isn't God good!" in response to
superficial blessings such as a beautiful home or a luxuri-
ous new couch. But if God is so good when I get a new
house, what does that make Him when my husband loses
his job?

Furniture, cars, or even houses do not define God's true
goodness. God does provide for all my needs in a wonderful way, but His love goes so much deeper than that.

It is in sending His Son to die for my sins, it is in making me His child through the waters of Baptism, it is in the forgiveness that is mine through His Supper, it is in His promise of eternal life because of His Son's resurrection that God's love and goodness find their true definition.

Dear Father,

Remind me that You are good ... always.
In Jesus' name. Amen.

Every good and perfect gift is from above,
coming down from the Father of the heavenly
lights, who does not change like shifting shadows.
James 1:17

Not My Son

I took deep breaths, trying to ease the tightness in my chest and keep the tears from running my mascara. I wanted to make a good impression on the principal, even if this wasn't the place I wanted my children to attend school.

As I drove to the local elementary school, I prayed, "God, if there is any way to send Mark to our church's school, show it to me. Please put Mark in the school that would be best for him."

As I turned into the school's parking lot, I felt better. I knew God would take care of Mark, even in the public school. Maybe God wanted him to be here. Maybe God wanted my child here so He could use Mark as a witness to others. I felt the tightness in my chest returning. My little boy wasn't equipped to go up against those who didn't believe. They could crush him.

I turned the car off but didn't get out. I sat in the parking lot and prayed, "God, I will do what You want me to do, but I don't want to sacrifice my son."

As I said those words, I shivered. I came to a new realization of the depth of God's gift to me. I wanted to hold back. I wanted to protect my son and keep him from being hurt in any way. I would rather go myself than send my children into uncertain circumstances. The thing I find so hard to give—my child—is the very thing God gave to me.

God didn't send His Son into uncertain circumstances. He sent Him into certain death. Even the worst outcome I could imagine did not come close to what God *knew* His

Son would endure. God loved me so much that He sent Jesus anyway so I could be saved. He gave me the ultimate gift, a gift I can't even imagine giving, the gift of His beloved Son. Because of this gift, because of Jesus' death on my behalf, I have forgiveness of sins. Because of Jesus' resurrection, I have the gift of eternal life.

Dear Father,

"Thank You" seems to fall so short when the gift is as costly and as valuable as Your gift of Jesus to me. But thank You for Your love, thank You for Your Son, thank You for Your sacrifice, and thank You for forgiveness and eternal life. In Jesus' precious name. Amen.

*For God so loved the world that He gave His one
and only Son, that whoever believes in Him
shall not perish but have eternal life.
John 3:16*

Kindergarten

I don't want to go to school!" Mark wailed. "I want to go home with you!"

I'd like to take you home with me, I thought as I looked at him, *but you need to go to school.* I had prayed about this decision and felt confident that this was the right school, the right teacher, and the right time for Mark. But that didn't make it easy for either one of us.

Mark clung to me with both hands as I tried to walk toward the teacher. Mrs. Ross smiled knowingly as she heard us coming. I had warned her that Mark was nervous. And she knew that I was nervous too. I wanted to stay for a while, but I knew the sooner I left, the sooner Mark would settle down. So I peeled Mark's hands from their grip on mine, placed his hand in Mrs. Ross' inviting hand, and made my exit.

"Mommy, I want you!" Mark yelled. I stiffened and kept walking. "Mommy! Mommy!" I walked out the door and around the corner. As far as he was concerned, I was gone, but I could still peek around the corner to see what was happening. The cries continued, "Mommy! Mom-meeee!" Even when I got home, his cries rang in my ears. I felt like I had abandoned my son.

I wondered if this was how Moses' mother felt when she placed her son in the river and walked away. Did she long to hold her son close and not let go? Did she think that it was all a big mistake and wonder why she had left him there? Did she have trouble concentrating on her daily tasks?

Or did she know that God held her baby in His hands? Did she trust that God had a plan, a beautiful plan, for her son? Did she believe that God intended for her to continue the work of raising this child?

Taking Mark to kindergarten is not as demanding a decision as placing a baby in a basket in a river to save his life. And Mark may never lead thousands of people. But God holds my child in His hands and has wonderful plans for him. He has made Mark His own through Baptism. God promises me that He will guard and protect my son. Although I feel lost for the moment with my child gone, God has given me the task to continue the work of raising this child to be His servant.

Dear God,

It is hard to let go of my son. Hold before me Your promises of protection and guidance. Give me an extra measure of Your Holy Spirit that I may continue to share Your Word and the Good News of Jesus with my children. Remind me that You are always with Mark and that You have a plan to use him in Your kingdom. In Jesus' name. Amen.

"For I know the plans I have for you," declares the LORD, "plans to prosper you and not to harm you, plans to give you hope and a future."
Jeremiah 29:11

I Don't Sew

ommy, you need to get on the ball and start sewing," Mark said as he met me at the end of the hallway.

I looked at my 6-year-old son bouncing up and down in front of me. His 4-year-old brother came up behind him in a show of support. Since when did they care if I sewed? And where had Mark come up with "on the ball"? I wasn't baffled for long. I took one step into the living room and looked at my friend sitting on the couch.

"The hem on his sleeve is coming out," she offered.

I looked her in the eye and without any tone of apology in my voice said, "I don't sew."

"That's what Steve said," my friend commented almost as an aside, then she busied herself with Mark.

I looked across the room at my husband and smiled. Steve probably had told tell her that I didn't sew. About a year ago, he had decided that a pair of his dress pants were not as long as he liked, but rather than give the pants away, he wanted to make them into shorts. So Steve informed me of this plan and laid them on the dresser. The pants lay there untouched until he cut and pinned them where he wanted them hemmed. Then he placed them back on the dresser. They collected dust until we went to his parents' house for the weekend. He took them along, and his mom made a pair of shorts for him. She also gave Steve a sewing lesson.

While those pants were collecting dust, I finished writing a book and started decorating a nursery. I cooked. I cleaned. I played chauffeur. I took children to the park, to swimming lessons, and to Grandma's. I went on dates with my husband and listened to him decompress after long days at work. I sat in the recliner with two boys nestled close and read countless stories.

I would like to be able to sew. Making my own clothes and recycling old clothes into new could save money. But I know that God has given me other gifts to use. He has given me the ability to write for Him. He has given me the ability to manage my house and to raise my children and to love my husband. These are ways He calls me to serve Him.

God doesn't expect me to sew or to conduct symphonies or to perform surgery. He has chosen other people to do these things. What He does ask is that in all my work, I work for Him. And He sends His Holy Spirit to guide my words and actions to reflect the new life in Jesus that I have been given. So even if I can't sew, others can see my love for God in the ways I use the talents He has given to me to accomplish the tasks He puts before me.

Dear Lord,

Help me use my gifts and abilities to accomplish the tasks You give to me. Guide me as I choose my activities. Use my words and actions to show Your love to others. Thank You for the gifts You have given me, and help me act as Your chosen child. In Jesus' name. Amen.

There are different kinds of gifts,
but the same Spirit. There are different kinds
of service, but the same Lord. There are different
kinds of working, but the same God works all
of them in all men. 1 Corinthians 12:4–6

Hidden Treasures

My friend Jan set the box labeled "Lindsey's Baby Clothes" in front of the couch. "I haven't had a chance to go through this one."

I was glad she had invited me to go through the box before the garage sale to see if there was anything I could use for Angela. We opened the lid and pulled out little pink dresses, pajamas with teddy bears, and adorable rompers. I began to make a pile of things I wanted to consider.

Then Jan brushed a thin piece of faded material with her fingertips. "Oooh, I remember this," she said and sighed. She held up a white cotton nightgown with a yellowish stain on the front. "Lindsey looked so cute in this one."

I smiled, knowing that my friend was seeing things that I couldn't. Although her daughter was now 9 years old, Jan was seeing her as a toddler, freshly bathed and ready for bed.

Although memories kept washing over her as she helped me unpack that box, Jan knew the time had come to clear out the baby stuff. Instead of hanging on to the past, it was time to make room for the future.

It's not easy for me to think about giving up my children's baby things either, even if they are stained or faded. So many of my memories are tied up in them. It's hard to let go of such treasures. But the real treasures are my children, not the memory of what they wore or how they looked. And the treasure I want most to share with them is heaven. I feel privileged to teach them about Jesus their Savior, about their heavenly Father who loves them completely, and about the Holy Spirit who strengthens the faith they have received.

Raggedy old clothes won't mean anything when my children, their father, and I are living forever in paradise.

Dear Father,

You have given me so many treasures, including my husband and my children. Thank You for giving all of us the most important treasure—faith in Jesus our Savior. We know this treasure can never be destroyed. Bring us all safely to You in heaven after years of living as treasures to one another here on earth. In Jesus' name. Amen.

"Do not store up for yourselves treasures on earth, where moth and rust destroy, and where thieves break in and steal. But store up for yourselves treasures in heaven, where moth and rust do not destroy, and where thieves do not break in and steal. For where your treasure is, there your heart will be also."
Matthew 6:19–21

Kindergarten Attitude

I pulled a sheet of paper from Mark's backpack as I sat down next to him at the kitchen table. "This is a good tree, Mark. Did you paint it today?"

He shoved a brownie in his mouth before mumbling, "No, yesterday. I made a book about an apple tree today."

"Oh, here it is," I said, pulling out his book.

"I made a sheep at school," Nicholas said, joining in the conversation.

"You don't go to a real school," Mark said. "I go to a real school. I'm in kindergarten. You're only in preschool."

I put the book down and looked at Mark. "Nicholas goes to a real school too," I said. "He is in preschool and that is exactly where he should be at this age. When he is older, he will go to kindergarten too."

I was surprised by Mark's attitude. I knew he felt important because he was in kindergarten, but he seemed to have developed an air of superiority. The amusing thing about his perception is that elementary-school children consider kindergartners to be the lowest of the low—the babies.

It's easy for me to take on a kindergarten attitude at times. I start thinking that I am important. I start to feel proud of my accomplishments. Like the proud Pharisee who thanked God that he was not like the miserable tax collector, I might even think I am better than others.

I want to list all my achievements and virtues, but in reality, I am nothing without Christ.

It's only because Jesus paid for my sins with His blood that I am even able to stand before God. Alone, I fall miserably short. It is Christ working in me that allows me to accomplish anything in God's eyes. Jesus makes me great.

Dear God,

Let me pray with the tax collector, "God, have mercy on me, a sinner." Forgive me for Jesus' sake. Amen.

May I never boast except in the cross of our Lord Jesus Christ, through which the world has been crucified to me, and I to the world. Galatians 6:14

Worry

I looked out the front window for the 20th time that hour. I stood staring down the street, hoping Steve might appear while I was standing there. Nothing. He was late, and I was worried. This wasn't like him.

As I folded socks, my mind drifted up the mountain where Steve was riding his bike. I could almost see him coming down a steep slope too fast. As he approaches the curve, his tires go through loose sand, losing traction. Now he and the bike slide across the road and off the edge of the cliff. Because I couldn't cope with the gory details that concluded that scene, I began to wonder how I would manage to care for three children by myself. How long would the insurance money last? Would that be enough time for me to get certified to teach again and to find a job?

When Steve finally arrived home, his story wasn't so dramatic. After his bicycle ride, he had returned to the car to find the lights on and a dead battery. He had to ride quite a distance to find a phone. Using his last quarter, he called for roadside assistance. Then all he could do was wait. When the battery was recharged, he came straight home to find his wife organizing a search party.

I had spent the whole afternoon worrying for nothing. To be honest, I do that often, though it doesn't do me any good. When I place Steve, or whatever else I might be worrying about, in God's hands, I have done more than if I fret and stew for hours.

In His Word, God reminds me that I can place all things into His hands. He invites me to come to Him with any request at any time. He promises to answer me. He knows what is best for me and my loved ones, even as He knew that we needed a Savior and sent Jesus to win us back from sin and death.

I'm learning to remember that God can take my worries and fears and replace them with peace and trust. I remind myself that when Steve goes biking, God goes with him. A prayer for his safety really does go a long way. Steve is precious to God and He will be there through the dead batteries or the accidents.

Dear Father,

> I am a worrier. Forgive me for my lack of faith
> and trust in You. Send Your Holy Spirit to remind
> me that You hold my family and me in the palm
> of Your hand, and we have nothing to fear.
> In Jesus' name. Amen.

*Do not be anxious about anything, but in every-
thing, by prayer and petition, with thanksgiving,
present your requests to God. And the peace of God,
which transcends all understanding, will guard
your hearts and your minds in Christ Jesus.*
Philippians 4:6–7

Oh, No! Not a Tower!

I t looks like Quincy won't be getting a knight's tower like yours for Christmas after all," I told Mark as I hung up the phone after talking to Quincy's mother.

Mark looked relieved. "Good."

"Don't you like your tower?" I asked, surprised by his reaction.

"Uh-huh."

"Then why don't you want Quincy to have one?" I asked.

"When I get something that my friend has or he gets something that I have, neither one of us plays with it anymore," he replied.

"So you think that if Quincy gets a tower for Christmas, neither one of you will play with your towers anymore?"

"Yeah."

His reasoning amused me. I couldn't convince him that two people owning the same toy did not make it outdated. He knew. He was speaking from experience. The trouble with Mark basing beliefs solely on experience is that he can be misled.

I can be misled too. Seeing God at work in my life or the lives of those around me is incredible. Even reading about how God brought about miraculous changes in people's lives is amazing. But I can't base my conclusions about God on something as earthbound as my physical senses. These will only offer a one-dimensional perspective. They will only tell me there is someone or something "in control." There's only one source for information about the one, true God.

That single source is God's Word. The Bible is the Word of God. The Bible is the truth. It tells us about a heavenly Father who created us; about Jesus, the Son of God, come to earth to save us from sin, death, and the devil; and about the Holy Spirit, who is sent to work faith in our hearts and to keep us in that faith. When everything around me seems to be based on superficial realities or changing whims, I can cling to the truth of God's Word. It never changes.

Dear Father,

Thank You for giving me Your Word. It is truly good to read and learn it, to digest it as sweetest honey. Let it be a light to my path. Remind me that Your Word never changes, especially Your Word of forgiveness, which is mine for Jesus' sake. In His name I pray. Amen.

*All Scripture is God-breathed and is useful
for teaching, rebuking, correcting and training
in righteousness, so that the man of God may be
thoroughly equipped for every good work.*
2 Timothy 3:16–17

Whom Are You Going to Listen To?

"Come on, Mark, or you will miss the bus!" I called into the house. "Get your lunch and backpack."

Mark came out with one arm in his jacket, his other hand reaching for the other sleeve. The backpack was hooked over his uncloaked arm, getting in the way. I took it from him so he could finish with his jacket.

"There's Lisa," Mark announced as the kindergartner from across the street and her mother started our way.

As I helped Mark put on his backpack, I realized that it was pretty light. "Did you get your lunch?"

"I couldn't find it."

I glanced at my watch and realized the bus could be down at the corner anytime. "You hurry to the bus stop. I'll get your lunch."

As he started to run, I saw his shoelaces flopping. I could visualize him sprawled on the sidewalk. "Mark," I called, "tie your shoes."

He bent down to tie his shoes, and I started inside to look for his lunch. I heard Lisa's mom call, "Mark, come on or you'll miss the bus."

I looked back and saw Mark jump up to run with his laces still dangling. "Mark!" Authority resounded in my voice. "Tie your shoes!"

He did, then raced down the street.

I retrieved the lunch and headed after Mark. I thought about how confusing this must have been for him. Two adults had been giving conflicting orders. To whom was he supposed to listen—the lady across the street or his mom? When the neighbor told him to come, it seemed right to obey so he wouldn't miss the bus. But I was more concerned with his safety. If he had missed the bus, I would have taken him to school. But if he had tripped on his shoelaces, he could have been hurt.

Just as so many different directives confused Mark, I get confused too. The wisdom of the world can seem to have merit at first glance, but God's Word often appears to be in conflict with the world. To whom should I listen—God or the world? Do I do what popular opinion tells me to do, or do I listen to what my heavenly Father says in His Word?

My heavenly Father created the world, loves me so much He sent His Son to suffer and die in my place, and cares enough about me to give me the gift of faith in Jesus so my sins are forgiven and I can live with Him forever in heaven. He cares deeply about what happens to me here on earth. When the messages of this world confuse me, I can trust my Father who loves me. He will send His Holy Spirit to help me make wise decisions.

Dear Father,

Send Your Holy Spirit to help me listen to You, especially when the world sends me conflicting messages. Thank You for the clear messages in Your Word, especially the ones about Jesus, my Savior. In His name I pray. Amen.

For the LORD gives wisdom, and from His mouth come knowledge and understanding. Proverbs 2:6

The Tip

If I have time, I will make milk shakes for dinner," I told Mark as I dumped the can of split pea soup in a pan. "And the best way for me to have enough time is for everyone to stay out of the kitchen."

"Stay out of the kitchen!" Mark hollered as he left the room. The kids played in the bedroom while I grilled the cheese sandwiches, warmed the soup, and made the milk shakes.

The whole purpose behind this menu was to get it on and off the table as quickly as possible so I could get to my meeting that night on time. It worked.

When I arrived home, the house was quiet. The children were asleep. Steve greeted me and said, "There's a note from Mark on the table."

Curious, I walked to the table. Mark couldn't read yet and was just learning a few words, so I knew even a short note would be quite an effort.

I opened the decorated envelope. Inside was a dime and a heart shaped note. On one side it read, "I love you, Mommy." On the other side it read, "Thank you for dinner."

I smiled as I slid the message and tip back inside the envelope. Usually preparing meals is a pretty thankless job. Everyone expects to have the meal waiting. When the food is not there, I hear complaints.

This episode made me consider all that I "expect" from God without really thinking about it ... until the items are not there. He supplies all kinds of wonderful things—like food and water and air to breathe and clothes and shelter and transportation—so regularly that I forget to thank Him unless they are exceptional or have been absent for a period of time.

So often when I go to God in prayer, I go with my needs list. What a pleasant idea to go with my thanksgiving list and delight Him in the same way Mark delighted me—with a special "thank You."

Dear God,

Thank You. Thank You for the magnificent things like creating me and saving me. Thank You for the beautiful things like my family and friends. Thank You also for the things that I take for granted like each breath I take. Thank You for everything. In Jesus' name. Amen.

Shout for joy to the LORD, all the earth.
Worship the LORD with gladness; come before Him
with joyful songs. Know that the LORD is God.
It is He who made us, and we are His; we are
His people, the sheep of His pasture. Enter
His gates with thanksgiving and His courts with
praise; give thanks to Him and praise His name.
Psalm 100

I Had Blown It Anyway

I put the groceries in the back of the car and grabbed the bag of chocolate-covered caramel peanuts. I tossed the candy on the seat beside me as I got into the car. Just before putting the car in reverse, I reached for nourishment for the long trip home from the grocery store.

A little voice inside my head said, "What about your diet?"

Then another voice said, "You already blew your diet at lunch. You may as well have the chocolate. You can start the diet over tomorrow."

It is always this second voice that gets me into trouble.

While the first voice urged me not to make the problem worse, the second voice argued that it didn't matter— I had already blown the diet. I ate the candy—not just one piece but two. I even sat inside the car inside the garage until I finished chewing so my children wouldn't know I had candy.

I allowed a past mistake to give me reason to fail again. Unfortunately, my spiritual life falls victim to this kind of faulty reasoning too. Sometimes when I am talking to God about a problem or need, a voice says, "How dare you ask for God's help after you disobeyed Him!" I feel inclined to let the guilt of past sins keep me from turning to God. But then the Holy Spirit reminds in the words of Scripture or comforts me with the reality of Christ's sacrifice for me, and I remember that God forgives my sins and wipes the slate clean. He wants me to come to Him with my concerns. There is nothing that can separate me from the love of God.

When I blow my diet, I try to see each new temptation as an opportunity to start with a clean slate. Each time I sin, God invites me to confess my sin and be forgiven. Through the forgiving work of Jesus, I am free to move forward with a clean slate. By the power of the Holy Spirit, I can do what I know God expects.

Dear God,

I have made so many mistakes and seem to keep repeating them. Please forgive me for Jesus' sake. Send Your Holy Spirit to help me move forward and keep me focused on the things ahead all the way to eternity. In Jesus' name. Amen.

Brothers, I do not consider myself yet to have taken hold of it. But one thing I do: Forgetting what is behind and straining toward what is ahead, I press on toward the goal to win the prize for which God has called me heavenward in Christ Jesus. Philippians 3:14

At Your Service

I slipped my hands under Angela's arms and lifted her from the high chair. I held her at arm's length as I headed straight for the bathroom. A mere washcloth would not handle this job. She needed to be immersed in water.

Just as I was drying Angela off, Nicholas came into the bathroom. "I want some more milk," he announced.

"Okay, as soon as I dry and diaper your sister." I wrapped Angela in a towel. With one arm around her, I grabbed a piece of toilet paper and wiped Nicholas' nose before he could get away from me.

I picked up a diaper, tucked it under my arm, and carried Angela to the living room. I worked to keep her on the towel until I could at least get the diaper fastened. She worked to get free so she could run through the house. I almost had the diaper on when a foot landed right next to the towel. I looked up to see Mark.

"Tie my shoe," he demanded.

"Please," I prompted.

"Please," he echoed.

"You tie one, and I'll tie the other," I said.

Mark agreed. While I worked on his shoe, I thought about all the tasks I needed to do today. The immediate ones included getting Nicholas some milk, dressing Angela, and packing Mark's lunch. Then I still had my regular chores such as laundry, dishes, and cleaning the bathroom.

Much of my time is spent meeting the needs of others, especially the needs of my children. I often feel like a servant. But when Jesus washed the disciples' feet, He was modeling servant behavior for them. He told them— He told us—to do the same.

When I prepare food, dress the children, or organize the household papers, I am doing as Jesus commanded. I am serving those around me. At times, I feel discouraged. It seems the duties I perform are meaningless. But the cooking, the cleaning, and the serving are all part of God's work. And God's work is not meaningless.

Dear Lord,
Much of the time, I feel like a servant. That doesn't feel honorable or dignified. Remind me that my service, in whatever capacity, honors You. In Jesus' name. Amen.

Whoever wants to become great among you must be your servant, and whoever wants to be first must be slave of all. Mark 10:43–44

Washing Hair

I lathered the shampoo in my hands and massaged it into Nicholas' hair and scalp while he played with his bath toys. Once I had the shampoo worked in, I reached for the handheld showerhead. This was the rough part.

I had been trying to convince Nicholas that if he looked up when I sprayed his hair, the water would run down his back. To him, looking up into the spray nozzle was like asking to be sprayed in the face. So he looked down, which brought all the water into his face and eyes.

I adjusted the water temperature and said, "Okay, Nick. It's time to rinse your hair. Look up at me."

To my surprise, he lifted his chin and looked in my direction. I trained the stream of water just behind his hairline, rinsing the shampoo from his hair and down his back. I held his chin in my hand, keeping his face tilted up. Once I finished rinsing his hair, I smiled. "There. Wasn't that easier? And I didn't get any water in your eyes," I commented.

Nicholas continued playing with his toys while I put the showerhead back in its holder. I felt like we had passed a milestone that day. He finally trusted me enough to do what I asked, even though it went against his instincts.

Instead of following God's directions, I often want to follow my natural instincts. The problem is, my natural instincts will lead me in the opposite direction God wants me to take. Because of sin, I can't trust myself to do what is right. But God has sent His Holy Spirit "to hold my chin up." He has worked faith in my Savior, Jesus Christ, in my heart and He continues to strengthen this faith every time I listen to or read God's Word and every time I eat Christ's body and blood at His Holy Meal. As I look at God through the clear eyes of faith, I see His wisdom and love and rejoice that He truly can be trusted.

Dear Lord,

Send Your Holy Spirit to strengthen my trust in You. Remind me that Jesus is the Way, the Truth, and the Life and that because of Him, I have nothing to fear. Thank You, heavenly Father, for showering Your gracious love on me and my family. In Jesus' name. Amen.

*"For My thoughts are not your thoughts,
neither are your ways My ways," declares the
LORD. "As the heavens are higher than the earth,
so are My ways higher than your ways
and My thoughts than your thoughts."
Isaiah 55:8–9*

Washing Hair Again

I was still feeling good about gaining Nicholas' trust when I started Angela's bath. After she had played for a while, I started shampooing her hair. I worked up a good lather in her hair, then took the showerhead to begin the rinse.

"Look at me, Angela," I said and started to spray the top of her head.

As soon as the water touched her head, she bowed her head. A steady stream of water and shampoo ran into her face. She started crying and rubbed her eyes with her hands.

I turned the nozzle away from her and wiped the water and shampoo from her face. "Look up at me and the water won't get in your face," I said. I lifted her chin into the same position that I had held Nicholas' earlier that evening. But when I tried again, she dropped her head to get away from the water, and again everything went right to her face. After several more tries, I finally got all the shampoo rinsed from her hair.

I dried Angela off, wrapped her towel around her, picked her up, and hugged her close. As I cuddled her, I thought about how God's lessons remain the same, the students just keep changing.

God has been training His people for thousands upon thousands of years. The Israelites had difficulty trusting His Word. King David had difficulty controlling his flesh. Peter had difficulty remaining faithful when the waters got rough. There is nothing I face that God hasn't seen before. The hurts that I have, the struggles, the fears—

God has seen them all. These difficulties are why He sent Jesus, His only Son, to this earth. Only Jesus has trusted perfectly, obeyed perfectly, remained faithful to the end—even a painful end on a cross in my place. And because Jesus suffered and died, I have forgiveness for the times I doubt. Because Jesus rose again, I have the faithful promise of my God that I have an eternal home with Him in heaven.

Nothing I come up against will surprise God. He has seen it before, and He knows how to handle it. I can trust Him completely.

Dear Father,

You have seen it all. Please be with me when
I come across something that I feel I can't handle.
Strengthen my reliance and trust in You. Forgive
me for the times I doubt. Point me to the cross,
where I see that You keep all Your promises.
In Jesus' name. Amen.

What has been will be again,
what has been done will be done again;
there is nothing new under the sun.
Ecclesiastes 1:9

Don't Give Up

I feel like giving up!" Steve said as he plopped sour cream on his baked potato. "Nothing seems to stick with these kids."

This wasn't the first time he had felt exasperated with his students. Every year brought at least a few junior high students that didn't show any interest in school or learning.

I put my fork down and looked at Steve. "It may not seem like anything is getting through, but you never know. Something you say or do may stick with these kids and make a difference in their lives years from now," I said.

Several weeks later, Steve came home from school in a particularly good mood. "One of my former students was on campus yesterday," he said. "He told the school counselors, 'If it hadn't been for Steve Duerr and Ken Kyle, I would have dropped out of school.' "

I turned from the sink to look at Steve. I didn't say anything—I just looked. He didn't seem puffed up or proud, just at peace.

"He's a senior in high school now. He says he has quit drinking and doing drugs. He is working at a fast-food restaurant and plans to go to the junior college next year," Steve added.

This was one of those students that Steve thought he wasn't getting through to. Apparently something got through. He stayed in school.

We were blessed to get a glimpse of the effect that Steve was able to have on one person's life, but we don't always have that opportunity. Who knows how the Holy Spirit may have used me during my years of teaching Sunday school and vacation Bible school? Who knows how the Holy Spirit may have used the words of God I shared at a Bible study or as an opening devotion? Who knows how the Holy Spirit blessed my public and not-so-public witnesses to my faith? Actually, someone does know. God knows.

When I convince myself that what I do is not of much consequence, that it doesn't matter, I remember that I won't know on this side of heaven how the Holy Spirit is using me. Although I may not see the results, I can trust God to use me in the ways He sees fit.

Dear Father,

Sometimes I feel frustrated because I feel as though the work I do is meaningless. Use me to share the Good News of Jesus, my Savior, with all those I meet. Remind me that nothing I do for You is ever meaningless. In Jesus' name. Amen.

Let us not become weary in doing good,
for at the proper time we will reap a harvest
if we do not give up.
Galatians 6:9

Think about Such Things

I sat, planted, on the couch, my teeth clenched together. Everyone else was in bed, where I should be, but I wasn't going. Steve was in bed, and I didn't want to be anywhere near him.

I fumed that he hadn't supported my plans. When he got home from work and I told him we were going to his parents' that night, I had anticipated some resistance. But it wasn't until it became obvious that we wouldn't get to his parents' until 1 A.M. or later that he decided we should wait until morning. I had worked hard organizing and packing since I had called his parents mid-afternoon to see if they would like guests. I didn't want to wait till morning.

I listed in my mind all the reasons I had to be angry with Steve. I soon realized that I wanted to be angry. I didn't want to let go of this. Bible verses kept popping into my mind, and I kept pushing them out. I was not in any mood to submit to my husband anyway. Then God reminded me of the verse that says, "Finally, brothers, whatever is true, whatever is noble, whatever is right, whatever is pure, whatever is lovely, whatever is admirable—if anything is excellent or praiseworthy— think about such things" (Philippians 4:8).

I tried to push this verse out too, but it wouldn't go away. So I begrudgingly relented. I went to my computer and typed out each adjective. Then I listed the things about my husband that fit each category. I was reluctant at first, but the more I thought about Steve's attributes, the easier it got—and the more I appreciated him. I finally quit when I couldn't get the columns on my computer to work right. Steve is my computer troubleshooter, so I typed "computer whiz" under "excellent" and saved the document to work on later.

When I went to bed, the knots in my stomach were gone and so was the soreness in my jaw. At that point, I thought I might actually be able to sleep. In focusing on the good things about Steve, rather than the things that had irritated me, I felt peace. I also realized again that even though we don't always agree, I have a pretty good husband.

Anger is one of the tricks Satan can use to make us ignore the many gifts God has given us. When my plans conflict with God's plans, I can easily forget His blessings, His promises, and His sacrifice of His Son. But God is "slow to anger and abounding in love" (Psalm 86:15). He will not allow my faults to blind Him to His love for me.

Dear Lord,

Sometimes I want to hold on to my anger and focus on all the negative things. Show me the good, beautiful, wonderful things that You have given me. Give me a thankful spirit. In Jesus' name I pray. Amen.

Finally, brothers, whatever is true,
whatever is noble, whatever is right,
whatever is pure, whatever is lovely,
whatever is admirable—if anything is excellent
or praiseworthy—think about such things.
Philippians 4:8

The Seat of Honor

Bobby tilted his head back and yelled, "Nick wants more pizza!" My son sat next to the birthday boy, waiting for his pizza to be delivered.

I wanted to laugh as I looked at the two boys. Bobby, dressed in a pirate costume from his pirate hat to his black boots, knew his place. He ruled the seas. Nicholas had the distinguished honor of being seated next to the captain of the party and reaped the benefits. It wasn't long before Nicholas had another piece of pizza on his plate.

It brought home the fact that the best seat, short of being the birthday boy, was next to the birthday boy. But there were only two seats next to Bobby.

The mother of John and James asked that her sons would be seated next to Jesus when He reigned in glory. I, too, would like the privilege of sitting next to Jesus when I am in heaven, just as I'm sure everyone else would like to be seated next to Him. But if Jesus turned down this request regarding two of His disciples, why would He choose me to sit next to Him? I believe I will be at the back of the crowd, jumping to catch a glimpse of Jesus as He passes by. Or if there are trees in heaven, I might pull a Zacchaeus to sneak a peek.

These flawed images put limits on a limitless God. I am not going to be in heaven jockeying for a position at God's table. I am not going to be in a crowd hoping for a mere glimpse of Jesus. Both of these ideas are bound by the confines of this world.

By the power of the Holy Spirit working through Word and sacraments, I have a one-on-one relationship with my Lord right now. I can turn to Him at anytime with anything and He is there, giving me His full attention. When I get to heaven, I will come face-to-face with Jesus. My accessibility to Him will even be greater than it is now, not limited by the scope of this world.

Dear Father,

Sometimes I try to limit You, heavenly Father, by putting on You the limitations of this world. Remind me that You are so much greater than my limited understanding. Because of Your dear Son's saving work on the cross, I look forward to that time when I will be able to know You in Your glory. In my Savior's name. Amen.

And I—in righteousness I will see Your face;
when I awake, I will be satisfied
with seeing Your likeness.
Psalm 17:15

A Little Rest, Please

With a pacifier in one hand and a blankie draped over my shoulder, I said, "Okay, Angela, it is time for a nap."

"Noooo!" she screamed and tried to run away.

I scooped her up and carried her to the crib while she twisted and kicked, trying to get free. I tried to put the pacifier in her mouth, but she grabbed it and tossed it down into the bed. She continued to yell as I put the blankie down and laid her on it. She shot up to a standing position and started feeding the blankie over the side of the crib. "Nap-nap," I said and quickly exited the room, pulling the door to an almost-closed position.

I went to the living room, sat down in a chair, and prayed, "God, please let her take a nap today. She doesn't want to miss anything, but if she doesn't sleep, she will be too tired and cranky to enjoy the park this evening."

The screams and calls for "Mom-meee" continued. Occasionally, I peeked through the crack in the door to make sure she was okay. I even went in a couple of times to reassure her and return the pacifier and blankie to her. Eventually, she fell asleep, and she was still asleep when Steve and the boys left for the park.

I have a tendency to react just like Angela when God wants me to rest. I run away, screaming, "No! I have too much to do!" Resting seems like being lazy, especially when I have piles of laundry, dishes stacked in the sink, and clutter all over the house. But God still wants me to rest. He even went so far as to invite me to cast all my burdens on Him so I could rest.

I can keep going until I drop, at which time I have no choice but to rest. But is this the wisest use of my time and energy? God invites me to rest for a reason—that I might better serve Him. Even Jesus took time from His busy schedule to go away by Himself to rest and pray. Balancing work and rest means I will be awake and ready when God places tasks before me to do.

Dear Lord,

With all the things I have to do, I sometimes forget to rest. Show me the many opportunities I have to rest, including relaxing in Your Word, dining at Your Table, and worshiping You in Your sanctuary. Refresh me during my periods of rest that I may accomplish all the tasks You place before me. In Jesus' name I pray. Amen.

There remains, then, a Sabbath-rest for the people of God; for anyone who enters God's rest also rests from his own work, just as God did from His.
Hebrews 4:9

The Mask

chatted with Nicholas as we sat in the doctor's waiting room. I looked toward the woman seated across from us, but as soon as I made eye contact, she looked away. A little later, I looked up to see her turn away from me again.

I started feeling self-conscious. She seemed to be watching us from the corner of her eye, almost in a disapproving way. Nicholas was chattering quite a bit, but he wasn't being loud. I thought I was on my best behavior too. I hadn't raised my voice to my son or talked in that stressed-out tone I sometimes use after a long day. I tried to dismiss the situation as being my imagination.

The next time it happened, I checked my blouse to make sure it was buttoned. Suddenly, I realized I had forgotten to ask Nicholas to take the underpants off of his head. The underpants were his mask. He could see out one leg hole while a tuft of hair stuck out the other leg hole. When he put on his mask, he was transformed into some kind of superhero. I had meant to have him take them off before we came into the doctor's office.

I leaned over to my superhero and whispered, "Nick, can I have your mask?"

He gave it to me and with all the dignity I could muster, I slipped it into my purse.

It's hard to believe that I sat in the waiting room talking to Nicholas without seeing the underpants on his head. I did look at him, but I looked past his clothing to the little boy I love so much.

When God looks at me, He really doesn't see all the mistakes I have made, all the imperfections I have, or all the goofy things I have done or tried on. He sees right through any masks I might put on to hide or to become something I am not. When God looks at me, He sees Jesus' righteousness. And because He sees Jesus' righteousness, He sees me—the little child He loves so much.

Dear Father,

It is so nice to know that no matter how foolish I look to everyone else, I am beautiful to You for Jesus' sake. Thank You for loving me so much that You sent Jesus to be my Savior. What a gracious Father You are. In Jesus' name. Amen.

But now He has reconciled you by Christ's physical body through death to present you holy in His sight, without blemish and free from accusation.
Colossians 1:22

"Go Welcome"

ay, 'Go welcome,' Angela," Nicholas coached as he got up close to Angela's high chair.

Angela laughed and swung her hand at Nicholas' face. He backed away as she swung and slapped the high chair tray.

Nicholas moved in close again. "Say, 'Go welcome!' "

I smiled as I rinsed off the lunch dishes and put them in the dishwasher. Nicholas had thanked Angela for giving him a cookie. Now he was trying to teach her to say, "You're welcome." But he was teaching her the phrase as he had learned it from Mark. So "Go welcome" was being handed down from brother to brother to sister, and none of them knew it wasn't quite right. It was tradition.

I love traditions. There's a comfort and familiarity, even a specialness, to doing things the way they have always been done. But just because things have always been done that way doesn't make them totally right. More important, it doesn't make every other way wrong.

My church is full of traditions, which I like. But that does not mean I can't go to a church that doesn't have stained-glass windows. My church has a large, beautiful pipe organ, but I can praise God accompanied by a guitar.

While traditions are comfortable, my faith is not ground-ed on these traditions. I enjoy my favorite hymns and style of worship, but it is the Gospel I grab onto with both hands. My comfort is the knowledge that God loves me enough to save me, which He did through the blood of His Son shed on the cross.

Dear Lord,

I enjoy worshiping You in "traditional" ways, but show me how to praise You whenever the opportunity arises, as long as the manner of my praise brings You glory. In Jesus' name. Amen.

"You have let go of the commands of God and are holding on to the traditions of men."
Mark 7:8

The Conference

Steve started the boys' baths while Angela played in her bouncer seat. I scraped Nicholas' leftover meat loaf into the garbage disposal and sighed. I knew our bed was piled with laundry ready to be folded and put away. I replayed my dinner conversation with Steve. His principal wanted him to go to a middle-school conference in San Francisco.

"I'll have the three kids all by myself for four days?" I asked.

"I told Tim that I had to talk to you first. I don't have to go," Steve said.

He didn't have to go, but he wanted to. Four days straight, all by myself. "Let me think about it," I said.

I was almost done with the dishes when Angela decided she was done bouncing. I shoved the strainer and a couple more glasses in the dishwasher, added the soap, and turned the knobs before rescuing her.

After feeding Angela and putting her to bed, I headed for the laundry, still feeling apprehensive about the possibility of Steve being gone for so long. Feeling the need to talk things over with someone, I decided to call my friend Jean. Her husband travels frequently. If anyone could advise me, she could.

I held the cordless phone between my shoulder and chin as I folded T-shirts. "You can do it," Jean said without hesitation.

"I can?" I took hold of the phone to make sure I had heard her clearly.

"If it gets hard, you know the first thing to do." Jean's voice was strong and sure.

"I do?" My mind raced—call a baby-sitter? Go out to dinner? Leave town? "What is the first thing I do?"

"Pray." Her one-word answer said everything I needed to hear. Even if Steve left, I wouldn't be alone. God would be there with me the whole time. When I felt like I couldn't manage, I could call on Him for help.

I realized that this is where I should have started in the beginning. I didn't have to wait until Steve left to pray. As I folded the rest of the laundry, I took my concerns to God. He gave me the confidence to tell my husband to go to the conference. "I know that even if things get hairy, I won't be alone. God will be with me," I told Steve.

Dear Father,

You are always with me, ready to help. Thank You for the promise to hear my prayers and answer in my time of need. I trust Your promise because You kept Your most important promise—to send a Savior. In Jesus' precious name. Amen.

"Have I not commanded you? Be strong and courageous. Do not be terrified; do not be discouraged, for the LORD your God will be with you wherever you go." Joshua 1:9

Doing Lunch

had been to Leigh-Anne's house. Everything was in order. It was more than in order, it was elegant. Now it was my turn to have her to my house. Suffice it to say, my house was less than elegant.

I looked at my watch. It was just about time to get Nicholas and Leigh-Anne's son, Parker, from preschool. Then Leigh-Anne would meet us at my house and the two moms and two sons would have lunch together. I had worked all morning to make the house presentable, but as I headed for the door, I saw the clutter covering the television. I considered dumping everything on the TV into a box and stuffing it in the garage, but I realized that would make the dust more apparent.

"If she doesn't like me the way I am, then I don't need her for a friend," I grumbled to myself. But my eye scanned the room in an attempt to see my house from Leigh-Anne's perspective.

When Leigh-Anne walked through my door, the only thing she saw was Parker. She didn't see the TV, the dust, or the clutter. I don't think she knew what color the couch was as she gathered Parker onto her lap and listened to him recount his day.

We had a wonderful visit and discovered we had much in common. To think I almost didn't invite Leigh-Anne and her son to my home. In fact, I had put it off for several weeks because it was so much work to get the house ready for guests. But that assumes my guests are coming to see my house.

The reason I invited Leigh-Anne and Parker for a visit was not to show off my house. It was an opportunity to get to know each other and to allow the boys to play. In opening up my home, I opened up my life and invited this almost stranger to get to know me.

Just as I didn't need to put on a show for Leigh-Anne, I don't need to put on a show for Jesus. In fact, I can't do anything to make myself worthy to entertain such a guest. Instead, Jesus enters my life and does all the cleaning. Because of His death on the cross, I am washed clean in His blood. All my sins are replaced with a clean robe of righteousness. And because of Jesus' resurrection, I will enjoy a new home in heaven with Him forever. What comfort to know I don't have to impress my Lord and Savior. Instead, I can focus on getting to know Him even better.

Dear Lord,

Thank You for looking with love on me, dear Lord. Thank You for the clean heart You gave me in the waters of Baptism. Send Your Holy Spirit to strengthen my faith and trust in You. Help me to open up my earthly home, even if it is not perfect, that I may share You with those around me through the gift of hospitality. In Jesus' name. Amen.

I want to know Christ and the power
of His resurrection and the fellowship of sharing
in His suffering. Philippians 3:10a

Missed Opportunity

s our children played together, Leigh-Anne and I got to know each other better. We discussed everything from bread machines to mothers' groups to kindergarten. Then the topic turned to my weekly Bible study.

"You really enjoy your Bible study?" she asked.

I answered her question without thinking. "Oh yes, it gives me a break from the kids and allows me to be with other adults."

Why did I say that? I do get a break and I am with other adults, but I acted as if it were some social club. That's not the reason I go. Was I afraid of what she might think of me? Did I think she wouldn't understand? Was I embarrassed?

Her question caught me off guard. My Bible study is more than a weekly gathering. I spend time daily reading the Bible and going over the lesson so I will be prepared when my group gets together. It crossed my mind not to go this year because the kids' schedules would keep me so busy and make it difficult to commit to another thing. But the Holy Spirit has been at work in my heart through this study of God's Word. I have grown through these studies. I have been encouraged and uplifted as well as instructed and reprimanded. No matter how difficult the scheduling issues, I need my Bible study.

Yet as valuable as this time in God's Word is to me, I stumbled when given an opportunity to testify about my faith. Someone was asking me about my relationship with God—a perfect opportunity to share all the Lord has given to me. But I had blundered. I hadn't expected the question and wasn't prepared with an answer.

This was a good learning experience. I realized how easy it would be to miss opportunities if I wasn't prepared. God showed me that He will open unexpected avenues to share my faith. He asks me to be ready with an answer.

Dear Lord,

Please forgive me for my weakness and uncertainty. Be with me and show me the opportunities You give me to share Your saving love in Jesus with others. In His name I pray. Amen.

But in your hearts set apart Christ as Lord.
Always be prepared to give an answer to everyone
who asks you to give the reason for the hope that
you have. But do this with gentleness and respect.
1 Peter 3:15

Still She Sings

s the choir stood to sing, my attention was drawn to Jill. During the past week, her husband had been diagnosed with cancer. He would be starting chemotherapy the next morning.

Such a reality seemed so overwhelming to me, so all-consuming. I marveled as Jill stood in front of the church with the choir and sang. She did more than sing though. It seemed to me that she sang with everything that was inside of her. She praised God from the depths of her being.

What a witness. In the face of grave uncertainty, she worshiped God with her soul. She was not naive to the situation. She had watched her sister-in-law fight, then lose, a nine-year battle with breast cancer. While her brother still grieved the loss of his wife, Jill now faced a battle in her own home. Still she sang.

During the months that followed, she couldn't do much as she watched the chemotherapy and the cancer take turns ravaging her husband's body. She stayed at his side, encouraging him and helping him through it. When his condition would allow, she was in church, worshiping God. Still she sang.

When things looked darkest for Jill, I wondered if my faith would be strong enough to survive such an ordeal. I wondered if I would be able to sing praises to God if I had to watch someone I love suffer. I had serious doubts.

As I was driving to the funeral of another friend's husband and again considering how much faith I did or didn't have, I realized how arrogant I was being. I was looking at faith as something I could do. It is not. My faith comes from God. He gives it to me. He strengthens it through His Word and Sacrament.

I imagine that Jill has had her share of doubts and struggles, but God is there. He provides the faith she needs for this ordeal. And still she sings.

Dear Lord,

When I face things that would take me to my knees, turn me to You for the strength to praise and trust You. Thank You for giving me the faith in Christ that I need. Thank You for holding me through the times that I don't think I can endure. In Jesus' name. Amen.

Let us fix our eyes on Jesus, the author and perfecter of our faith, who for the joy set before Him endured the cross, scorning its shame, and sat down at the right hand of the throne of God.
Hebrews 12:2

No Tears Allowed

ngela's fever was down to 103 degrees when I carried her into the doctor's office. She was feeling better since I cooled her off from the 105 degrees it had been in the morning. But her fever had taken its toll on me. I dropped the diaper bag into a chair and carried Angela with me up to the front desk. As I signed her in, the receptionist joked, "You look worse than she does."

I couldn't hold in the tears. They started streaming down both cheeks. Suddenly concerned, the woman said, "We'll get you right into a room."

Once we were in the examining room, I composed myself, only to lose that composure when the nurse came in. A little later, there was a knock on the door and the doctor poked her head inside the room. "Is it safe?" she asked.

I smiled, feeling a bit embarrassed. "Did they warn you?"

"They warned me," she said as she came into the room and closed the door.

"I told myself all the way here that I wasn't going to cry." I could feel the tears coming again.

"Why not? If you can't cry here, where can you cry?" she asked as she hugged me.

Why not? Because I really didn't want to look like a blubbering idiot. I wanted to look like a woman who had a source of strength on which to lean. This doctor knows that I am a Christian. I wanted her to see that faith in action. I wanted her to see someone who trusted in God. I wanted to let my light shine.

The problem was that I was trying to handle Angela's illness with my own strength rather than God's strength. I was trying to wear my Christian faith as a fashionable piece of clothing. I was trying to prop God next to me instead of leaning wholly and completely on Him.

Dear God,

Remind me that I don't have to do and can't do everything by myself. But You have done all that is necessary to assure my heavenly victory through the death and resurrection of Your Son. Strengthen me when I am weak. Uphold me in times of crisis. For Your Son's sake. Amen.

But He said to me, "My grace is sufficient for you, for My power is made perfect in weakness." Therefore I will boast all the more gladly about my weaknesses, so that Christ's power may rest on me. 2 Corinthians 12:9

Behind the Scenes

T he first thing we heard as we entered the church were the songs that the vacation Bible school students had been learning all week. We hurried to find good seats before taking in the rest of the sights and sounds. Steve and the boys sat in one of the pews. I followed, carrying Angela. I tried to see the slides from the previous week as I made my way to the pew.

Just as I was about to sit down, I saw my friend Louise. We chatted for a few moments, then she asked if I saw the young woman with the braids and the guitar?

I looked in the direction that she had nodded. Between 15 and 20 children sat on the floor in front of the altar. In the middle of this group was a lady with two braids down her back. She was playing the guitar and encouraging the children to sing with her. I didn't know her, but I recognized her as a fairly new member of our church. I had seen her teaching Sunday school and vacation Bible school, as well as participating in other church activities. I turned back to Louise and nodded.

"Some time ago, she called when I was helping in the church office and asked for a ride to church. She said her husband worked weekends and she didn't have a car," Louise said. "I picked her up and arranged for others to help too. I wasn't very happy about it." She glanced at the woman with the guitar. "There is a lesson for me here."

I took Louise's confession with me and thought about what God had worked through her. Louise may have begrudgingly met the need of this woman—the seemingly insignificant act of providing transportation. In doing so, she took part in another person's ministry. Louise had not taught vacation Bible school, but even in her absence, she touched the lives of countless others.

I was encouraged by Louise's testimony. So much of what I do seems mundane and insignificant. But if God uses small, ordinary things that I do for others to allow them to soar, I can rejoice in their accomplishments.

Dear Father,

Show me the many ways You use me to accomplish Your work, even when the tasks seem mundane, tiresome, or inconvenient. Use me to proclaim the Good News of Jesus' saving work to all whom I meet. In Jesus' name. Amen.

*Therefore, my dear brothers, stand firm.
Let nothing move you. Always give yourselves
fully to the work of the Lord, because you know
that your labor in the Lord is not in vain.
1 Corinthians 15:58*

Little League Mom

I sat in the front row of the bleachers just behind home plate. The score was tied, and Mark was on third base. I gripped my pencil as the batter swung at the ball and missed. I held my comments, remembering that the ballplayers were only 7 years old. I marked the strike, then tapped the pencil against the scorebook.

Another pitch. Another swing. A hit! The ball went right between the shortstop and the third-baseman. Mark started running for home.

"Go! Go!" I screamed. Mark was close to home when the left-fielder threw the ball toward the plate. *They're going to throw him out,* I thought. Maybe Mark would ease up when he saw the ball coming home, but he kept barreling toward home. I jumped to my feet. "Run, Mark! Run!" I screamed.

He stepped on home plate just before the catcher could tag him.

"Safe!" the umpire called.

"Yea!" I yelled. "Way to go, Mark!"

I sat down and beamed as I noted the run in my book. You would have thought it was the World Series, the way I had cheered.

It wasn't the World Series, but Mark played to the best of his ability. He ran for home with everything he had and didn't hesitate when the ball came his way. That would have been enough reason for me to cheer, even if he had been tagged out.

It is difficult to imagine God in heaven cheering for me, yelling, "Go, Cathy! Go!" But in Luke 15 it says, "There is rejoicing in the presence of the angels of God over one sinner who repents." So there is cheering when I confess my sins and seek forgiveness for Christ's sake. God's encouragement and constant presence can keep me going, even when it looks like trouble is headed my way. Even when it looks like I might be tagged out, I can run for home without hesitating.

At the end of the season, Mark received a trophy featuring a gold-colored plastic baseball player. At the end of my earthly season, I will receive a crown that will last forever.

Dear God,

Help me to hear Your cheers and encouragement as I read Your Word. Send Your Holy Spirit to help me run for home. In Jesus' name. Amen.

Do you not know that in a race all the runners run, but only one gets the prize? Run in such a way as to get the prize. Everyone who competes in the games goes into strict training. They do it to get a crown that will not last; but we do it to get a crown that will last forever. 1 Corinthians 9:24–25

Extra Tickets

I sat on the couch and opened Nicholas' backpack, "Did you make any pictures in kindergarten today?"

"Uh, yeah. And there's a painting from yesterday in there too," he said.

I pulled out a painting of a bear holding a balloon and a construction-paper clock. Then I noticed his lunch tickets. I pulled them out to put them in a safer place.

"Nicholas, how come there are only three lunch tickets?"

"The lady was nice, she gave me extras."

"Extras?" I asked. "I gave you a check to get five tickets. You should have used one today and had four more."

"She gave me five."

"Well, there are only three here," I pointed out.

"I gave one to a girl on the bus."

"You gave one to a girl on the bus? Why?" I asked.

"She asked me for it."

"Who was it?"

"I dunno," he answered.

I put my head in my hands, sighed, and thought about what had transpired. I realized that I had never explained to him that the check was enough for five lunches. He thought the lunch ladies were kind and had given him extra tickets. So Nicholas generously passed on this kindness.

I felt frustrated with Nicholas, but I imagine that God smiled on him. I wanted to teach my son responsibility and that those tickets have value. God was watching one of His children give freely—the same way He wants me to give.

If I were wise, I would forget about the monetary value of the ticket and cherish the kindhearted spirit God has given to my son.

Dear Lord,

Although I don't want to, I sometimes get caught up in the materialism of the world. Help me to grow beyond mere responsibility into a loving, sharing person who knows You are the provider of everything—food, shelter, clothes, and most important, my salvation. In Jesus' name. Amen.

Give to everyone who asks you, and if anyone takes what belongs to you, do not demand it back.
Luke 6:30

Planning a Date

climbed into the car and looked back at the front porch to see Angela standing with my friend Jean. She waved and chanted, "Bye-bye, bye-bye." I waved at them. The boys already had gone back to playing with their friends.

"So where are we going?" Steve asked as he started the engine.

"I don't know," I said with a sigh. "How about going to the coffee shop and getting some extra-crispy french fries and a milk shake?"

"Sounds good," he said, and we started off on our date.

So we could have these dates, Jean and I exchange baby-sitting. We sit down with a calendar and pick out days—sometimes months in advance. Usually neither one of us has big plans for these evenings; we just need to spend time alone with our husbands.

Steve and I often go somewhere for shakes and fries, take a bike ride, or do some window shopping. But we always talk—uninterrupted. So often the responsibilities of home and work leave us with little time together. When we go out on dates, we set aside daily responsibilities and make each other a priority—before there is a crisis.

This time together is important because it gives us the opportunity to maintain our marriage and make it even stronger. The same holds true for my relationship with God. I need to make time, even set a date, to spend with God. One of those dates is Sunday morning when I gather with my family and my family of faith around Word and sacraments. But I also need time with God each day. As a busy mother, this is not an easy task. But as with Steve, I schedule it and preserve that time as a priority.

Uninterrupted time with God spent studying His Word allows the Holy Spirit to strengthen my relationship with my heavenly Father. As I grow in this relationship, I learn to lean on God and trust Him implicitly. Taking time from daily responsibilities to make God a priority helps me prioritize my other tasks and actually accomplish more.

I value my relationship with my husband and am willing to work to keep it healthy. I also value my relationship with my God. What joy to know that through study of His Word and participation in His Supper, this relationship is strengthened.

Dear God,

Help me to keep You as the focus of my life. Send Your Holy Spirit to strengthen my faith and trust in You. In Jesus' name. Amen.

You will seek Me and find Me when you seek Me with all your heart. Jeremiah 29:13

Longing

I sat in a little chair by Mark's desk in the first-grade classroom at back-to-school night. The room seemed blurry through my tear-filled eyes. Student work was displayed everywhere: little stories written on paper dresses and pants, dominoes depicting how many people were in each child's family, and writing journals on every desk. I was finally getting to see some of what Mark had been doing with the bulk of his time for the last several weeks.

Although the teacher came with an excellent reputation, I was feeling resentment toward school. As she talked about her desire for open communication between home and school, the tears spilled down onto my cheeks. I wiped them away, thinking only about how much I missed my son.

Mark was adjusting to first grade, but I wasn't. He was gone almost all day and when he did come home, he often had homework. I wanted my son. I wanted to sit and hold him and hear about all the wonderful things he was thinking. I wanted to play games with him, read with him, and take him places. Now I found myself trying to squeeze all these things in after school and before bedtime. There wasn't enough time.

Just as I desire that special time with my son, God desires special time with me, His daughter. There are so many things that take me away from Him, but He always pulls me back, inviting me to share my day with Him in prayer, inviting me to read His love letter to me—the

Scriptures. God longs to hold me. And because of Jesus' saving work on the cross and the Holy Spirit's gift of faith in Jesus, God does hold me close. And no one can take me from Him. Because of Jesus' resurrection, I will find myself in the most amazing place when I die—a heavenly mansion.

Dear Father,

I come to You seeking Your forgiveness for the things I allow to separate me from You. Thank You for sending Jesus to bridge the gap between us. Keep me close to You. In Jesus' name. Amen.

"O Jerusalem, Jerusalem, you who kill the prophets and stone those sent to you, how often I have longed to gather your children together, as a hen gathers her chicks under her wings, but you were not willing." Matthew 23:37

Let the Sun Stand Still

I slipped out of bed and made my way to the bathroom. The sun wasn't up yet, but I didn't turn on any lights until I closed the bathroom door. I wasn't ready for anyone else to get up. I had too much work to do.

As I headed for the living room, I was tempted to skip my morning Bible study time. There were so many things that I needed to accomplish—laundry, cleaning the bathroom, and mopping the floors. Today was the only day I would be home.

No, I thought, *I have been asking God to help me put Him first in my life.* For me, this included starting my day with Him. And if God could make the sun stand still in the sky so Joshua could finish his job, then God could help me find the time to complete the tasks that needed to be done.

I sat down and opened my Bible. In the still quiet of early morning, I spent some time alone with God. During that time, I presented my "to do" list to Him and asked for His guidance to do what was important. I also asked for the time to complete my tasks.

Later that morning, as I looked back on what I had already accomplished, I was amazed. All three children had slept in, which gave me extra time to clean the appliances. Angela splashed in the tub long enough for me to scrub the toilet and sink. I even spent time with my children.

God didn't "reward" me for doing my Bible study. But because I spent time with God, I was able to share with

Him my concerns and ask for help in ordering my day. Maybe this is why Jesus spent time by Himself, talking with God. It was an opportunity to focus, recharge, and plan.

God invites me to place my life in His hands. In one way it's already in His hands—because my Savior's hands were nailed to the cross in my place, I have received salvation and life. Knowing that I am so important to God means I can trust that He will help me with my earthly needs even as He helped me with my greatest spiritual need.

Dear God,

Sometimes I get so busy I think that I don't have time for You. Remind me that You are always with me to help me accomplish more than I could ever do alone. In the busy-ness of my life, help me to share Your love and peace with those around me. In my Savior's name. Amen.

But seek first His kingdom and His righteousness,
and all these things will be given to you as well.
Matthew 6:33

Just a Smudge

The kids and I hadn't been at my mom's house long when she said, "Come here. I want to show you something."

I followed her the entire length of her immaculate house. We went down the hall where pictures of my children graced the walls, then through the bedroom and past the neat, tidy dresser. When we reached the master bathroom, my mom gestured to the full-length mirror. A couple feet from the floor, right in the middle of the mirror, was a perfect little handprint. "It has been here since the last time you were here," she said.

"Oh, Mom, I'm sorry," I said, turning to go get the glass cleaner.

"Don't worry about it. I could have cleaned it, but I left it there on purpose."

I turned to see her smiling. She was proud of her little handprint. I had seen it only as something marring an otherwise clean room. She looked at it through the eyes of love and saw a treasure.

This is how God looks at me. At times, I imagine myself as a smudge on the beautiful world that God created, but God sees me through the eyes of love. He looks at me through the cleansing blood of Jesus' righteousness. I am no longer a spot to be removed, but a precious treasure that God has saved.

Dear God,

I am so glad that You love me so much, even though I don't deserve it. Thank You for sending Jesus to suffer and die in my place so I can be forgiven. Thank You that through Jesus' resurrection, I will be with You in paradise forever. In Jesus' name I pray. Amen.

When I consider Your heavens, the work of Your fingers, the moon and the stars, which You have set in place, what is man that You are mindful of him, the son of man that You care for him?
Psalm 8:3–4

What Really Makes Me Special

My patience was already paper-thin when I sat down at the table to help Nicholas with his schoolwork. I had over-committed again. I felt like I was being pulled in every direction. There were so many things to do, I wasn't doing anything well. I was so discouraged I hadn't wanted to face the day. But staying in bed was not an option. I had moved through my day with a mood of discouragement and worthlessness seasoning everything I did.

Now, Nicholas had been named "Star of the Week" in kindergarten. We needed to fill out some papers about who he was, then gather some pictures for him to display. Normally I would have enjoyed this assignment. But today it was just another task to be endured.

I picked up the pen to write his answers in the small blanks. "I want to write it!" Nicholas demanded. I sighed and got up to load the dishwasher. I rinsed dishes and spelled "green" while Nicholas wrote tiny, illegible letters.

We worked our way through the two pages. I read the questions, explained them, then spelled the words he wanted to write while he took the dictation. We finally arrived at the last question: "What really makes me special is ..."

Without hesitating, Nicholas answered, "Mom."

I tried to be patient, knowing that we were almost done. "Your teacher wants to know what makes you special. What is something special about *you*?" I asked.

"Mom. M-o-m." He wrote on his paper before I could suggest that he think of some special ability or quality that sets him apart.

"How do I make you special?" I asked.

"You hug me," he answered.

I was quiet for a moment while I thought about my 5-year-old's wisdom. He was special, not because of anything he had done or any personality traits but because he was loved.

The timing of his insight was perfect. It reminded me that I am special too. My self-esteem was at a low that day, but he reminded me that I am valuable, not because of what I can do but because of who loves me—God. In fact, He loves me so much that He sent His only Son to save me from sin, death, and the devil. That's an amazing love from an amazing God.

Dear heavenly Father,

Sometimes I feel worthless. Remind me that You loved me enough to sacrifice Your only Son for me. If You were willing to do that, I can't possibly be worthless. Thank You for loving me. In my Savior's name. Amen.

May our Lord Jesus Christ Himself and God our Father, who loved us and by His grace gave us eternal encouragement and good hope, encourage your hearts and strengthen you in every good deed and word. 2 Thessalonians 2:16–17

Under Attack

Angela's block city kept growing as she thoroughly enjoyed her time in the church's nursery.

The little boy who sat across the table from her was not enjoying himself. In fact, he seemed to be in a sour mood. He kept throwing blocks at Angela's creation. It looked like he was trying to knock down her city. But the foam blocks didn't fly well, and his ammunition fell short.

Then I realized that each time he threw a block, Angela laughed, reached over her city, and picked up the piece he had sent flying her way. She would use it to build on to her wall or add another building. She seemed to have no clue that he was not throwing the blocks *to* her to share but *at* her to knock down her masterpiece.

If I had been Angela in that situation, I would have become irritated. In fact, it seems that lately a lot of disagreeable circumstances have been thrown my way. I feel like stomping off to a corner and crying.

But Angela's example has made me consider an alternate attitude. Now, as I look at the things that get tossed my way, I ask God to show me how I can use them to build. Are these opportunities my heavenly Father has placed in my life so I will rely more on Him and less on myself?

Although I still want to run and hide from difficulties, I am asking the Holy Spirit to give me an attitude like Angela's. I want to see each struggle as a potential building block. Instead of sitting in a corner, feeling sorry for myself, I ask God to show me how He is using the trials

of my life for good. Daily I thank God that He is building
me into the person He needs for His kingdom.

Dear heavenly Father,

I do not like going through the bad times in life.
Remind me that You love me and only want good
for my life. Show me that even in these dark times,
You are with me, lighting the way. Even as Jesus'
disciples were devastated by His death, only
to rejoice three days later at His resurrection,
point me to the glorious future that awaits me in
heaven because of Jesus' saving work on the cross.
In His name I pray. Amen.

*You intended to harm me, but God intended it
for good to accomplish what is now being done,
the saving of many lives. Genesis 50:20*

Jesus' Yoke

I n my Bible, I read, "For My yoke is easy and My burden is light." I smiled as I remembered the time long ago when I learned how easy and light Jesus' burden really is.

I shifted the weight of my sleeping baby as I opened the apartment door. Steve looked up from typing job applications, then went back to his work without saying anything. I carried Mark to the bedroom and put him in his crib. Situating his blankie, I slipped out without waking him up.

With Mark asleep in the bedroom, there was no place for me to go but the living room—where Steve was. When I walked in this time, he didn't even look up from his work. I ached inside. I didn't know what to say to him. It seemed every time we tried to talk, we argued.

Instead, I collapsed on the couch, feeling alone. This was our lowest point as a married couple. Steve's graduate school had taken all the money we had and then some. Now he was done with school, but we were in debt up to our eyeballs. And the worst part was that we couldn't lean on each other.

I picked up my Bible. I knew that God was not in favor of divorce, but I wanted to see if there might be some loophole I could use.

I didn't find the loophole I was looking for, but over the next several months, I spent a lot of time in God's Word. Consequently, instead of leaving, I stayed—not because I wanted to, but because I was certain that was what God wanted from me. There were plenty of difficult times, but talking with a marriage counselor and studying the Bible were only two of the many steps we took as we struggled through that time in our lives.

Now I think I have a better understanding of what Jesus means when He encourages me to take His yoke because it is easy and the burden light. Following Jesus was much easier than striking out on my own. He pulled me through the rough spot in my marriage. Taking Jesus' yoke saved me from the heartache of a divorce. Carrying His burden has given me, among other blessings, a supportive husband whom I love so very much and not just one, but three beautiful children.

Dear Lord,

There are times that I don't feel like doing what You want me to do. There are times when it seems easier or more advantageous to do things the way I want to. In those times, remind me of Your promises. Remind me of all You have done through Jesus for me. Help me to be faithful to You and to the promises I have made. In Jesus' name. Amen.

"Come to Me, all you who are weary
and burdened, and I will give you rest.
Take My yoke upon you and learn from Me,
for I am gentle and humble in heart,
and you will find rest for your souls.
For My yoke is easy and My burden is light."
Matthew 11:28–30

A Valuable Treasure

I picked my way through the living room, gathering toys, books, and clothes along the way. I had to smile as I started to put Angela's favorite book back on the shelf. I had to admit it was fun. But after reading it over and over, I was in the mood for something different. So instead of putting it at the end of the shelf, I hid it in the middle. Just for a while, I thought to myself.

Later I walked into the living room and found Angela standing by the shelf in a pile of books. She turned around and grinned at me, holding up her treasure.

"Did you find your doggie book?" I asked.

She thrust it toward me.

"Shall we read it?" I smiled, more at the determination of my little girl than in delight that I would get to read that book again.

She climbed out of the pile and ran to me as I sat on the couch. She crawled into my lap, and we read about the doggies ... again.

Angela had found something good, and she was determined to hold on to it. I can learn from her example. I have found a treasure worth holding on to also—my relationship with my Lord. The Bible says, "The kingdom of heaven is like treasure hidden in a field. When a man found it, he hid it again, and then in his joy went and sold all he had and bought that field" (Matthew 13:44). This man stopped at nothing to make that treasure his.

I have a treasure. Jesus bought this treasure for me with His death and resurrection. But so often, I let the minor details of life loosen my grip on this treasure. But God doesn't let me fall. He sends His Holy Spirit to strengthen my faith and keep me on the path of righteousness. He will never let me go.

Dear Lord,

Send Your Holy Spirit to keep the things of
this world from separating me from You.
Help me to seek You and Your kingdom always.
In Jesus' name. Amen.

Praise be to the God and Father of our Lord Jesus Christ! In His great mercy He has given us new birth into a living hope through the resurrection of Jesus Christ from the dead, and into an inheritance that can never perish, spoil or fade—kept in heaven for you, who through faith are shielded by God's power until the coming of the salvation that is ready to be revealed in the last time. 1 Peter 1:3

Come, Let Us Adore Him

No one knew exactly what would happen. That was the delight of it.

The pastor retold the Christmas story using small children as his props. The 5-year-old "Mary" did indeed look sweet and pure. The pastor lifted the 3-year-old angel onto a chair to make her proclamations. And the littlest lamb in the flock was our 2-year-old Angela.

Angela looked so precious in her cotton ball-covered T-shirt and headband with the pointed, felt ears. I beamed as I watched my baby, hoping that she wouldn't get scared and come back to sit with us in the second pew. But she was oblivious to the church full of people. All she wanted was to see Baby Jesus.

When the pastor lifted the angel off her chair after announcing Jesus' birth, the shepherds started their journey to the stable, and the sheep followed. By the time they got to the manger, none of the little lambs could see around the bigger shepherds. But Angela wanted to see Baby Jesus.

Angela turned sideways and slid between two of the shepherds. She squeezed her way around Mary and Joseph to the front of the manger. As she arrived, her brother and the other two wise men were arriving to kneel before the King. Angela knelt also and could barely see over the top of the manger where the child was sleeping.

Angela, in her 2-year-old wisdom, focused on what was truly important at Christmas. I had been preoccupied with balancing the children's Christmas presents, buying groceries for Christmas brunch, and wrapping the last gifts. I had gotten lost in the production of Christmas. Angela was intent on seeing Baby Jesus. In her childlike way, she reminded me that Christmas was for worshiping Baby Jesus.

Dear heavenly Father,

Remind me that Christmas is not giving and receiving gifts, eating good food, and being charitable. It is the celebration of Your Son's birth. Help me to praise and worship the King. In Jesus' name. Amen.

"I tell you the truth, anyone who will not receive the kingdom of God like a little child will never enter it."
Luke 18:17

What a Gift!

T he boys just about flew into Grandma's house and Angela toddled in after them. They were anxious to check out the Christmas tree and see the presents underneath.

One present in particular caught everyone's attention. Perhaps it was the flashing lights wrapped around it. Perhaps it was the strange red shape, which, in addition to the lights, was also adorned with bows and candy.

Mark looked at the present and read the tag: "To Mark and Nick from Uncle Don."

Uncle Don always gives imaginative and fun gifts. The boys couldn't wait to find out what was in that package. It was the first present they wanted to open.

After removing the lights, bows, and candy, they tore into the paper and found a basketball and another present. With barely a glance at the ball, Mark grabbed the package to unwrap it, revealing a football and another present. "I want to open this one!" Nicholas complained. So Mark handed it to him to unwrap. Each time they opened a present, something was revealed while something else remained wrapped. Neither boy seemed to pay much attention to what they received, they were more focused on unwrapping the next package.

Sometimes I am like this too. I am so focused on what might be coming next that I completely forget about all the wonderful gifts I already have received.

Watching my sons with their present, gave me the opportunity to reflect on all that God has so richly given to me—my family, my friends, my home, my faith. And even with all this, I can trust my heavenly Father to provide all my earthly needs even as He has satisfied my need for salvation through the death and resurrection of His Son.

Dear Father,

Thank You for giving me so much. I truly am rich. In Jesus' name. Amen.

I know what it is to be in need,
and I know what it is to have plenty.
I have learned the secret of being content
in any and every situation, whether well fed
or hungry, whether living in plenty or in want.
Philippians 4:12

It Takes Time

"How long have you two been married?" Earl asked Steve and me as we played golf with our new friends.

"Three years," Steve said as he teed up his ball.

Earl smiled at his wife. Leaning on his driver, he said, "I don't believe anyone is really in love until they've been married for 13 years."

"Oh, really?" I said and laughed. "How long have you been married?"

"Thirteen years." He answered with only the slightest hint of a smirk.

I didn't say anything. Steve and I just exchanged a smile.

This little scene was amusing at the time, but as Steve and I approach our 13th anniversary, I can see a lot of truth in Earl's words.

When we were first married, we were still in that infatuation stage. It has taken time for our love to grow into what we have today. Together we have been through births and deaths, successes and disappointments, dreams and failures. Through the highs and lows, we have learned more about those hidden places in both of our hearts and have learned more about what each other needs.

I'm not sure there is anything magical about 13 years, but it does take time for a relationship to mature.

Likewise, it takes time for my relationship with God to mature. Not from God's part, He has already given everything, including His precious Son, who died on the cross for my salvation. But it takes time for the Holy Spirit to prepare me to use the gifts God has given to me. It takes time for the Holy Spirit to develop that childlike trust in God in my heart so I will share everything with my heavenly Father.

When I married Steve, I knew that I loved him. And three years later I still loved him. But 13 years later, I can see how all that we have been through together has deepened that love into something I never could have imagined the day I said, "I do."

I love God. Each day with which He blesses me deepens that love into something greater than I can even imagine.

Dear Lord,

I say, "I love You," and I do. But I know that You will send Your Holy Spirit to deepen that love in my heart. Help me to spend time with You in Your Word and in the fellowship at Your Table so my faith and love will grow. In Jesus' name. Amen.

Then we will no longer be infants, tossed back and forth by the waves, and blown here and there by every wind of teaching and by the cunning and craftiness of men in their deceitful scheming.
Ephesians 4:14

Urged by the Spirit

We pulled into the driveway after our trip to the medical lab. The tech had drawn Angela's blood ... again. I felt defeated. I had hoped that the high fevers would go away; instead, they were coming more frequently. I wasn't the one who was sick, but the emotional drain fatigued me.

I grabbed the mail on the way in to the house. Sitting down on the couch with Angela, I rifled through the envelopes. I smiled as I saw one from Margie. Actually, it was from my in-law's church, but I knew Margie was the one who sent the cards. I had met her once. Setting the rest of the mail aside, I tore open the envelope and read the card and the message she had written. I felt as though God were there, talking to me, encouraging me, and reminding me that He was in control.

He did hold Angela in His hand. He knew the drain those fevers had on her and on me. He supplied us with the strength we needed to make it through. Sometimes that strength came from unexpected sources, like Margie, who shared His Words of love and encouragement in Jesus with us.

Margie had no idea Angela would be sick the day I received her card. When I had met her, she told me that she sends her cards when the Holy Spirit prompts her to. Obviously, God knew my needs and took care of me— even as He knew my greatest need for a Savior and sent Jesus to this earth for me.

Since that time, I have reflected on Margie's simple action and how it affected me so deeply. I have also thought about the times the Holy Spirit urges me through God's Word to take action. What tremendous opportunities God places before me to serve Him by serving others. He will bless even the simple card that tells someone I'm thinking about her and praying for her.

Dear Lord,

Send Your Holy Spirit to help me do Your will
and to serve You in the ways You know best.
Thank You for the gift of friends who share Your
love with me. Thank You for my best Friend—
Jesus. In His name I pray. Amen.

Since we live by the Spirit,
let us keep in step with the Spirit.
Galatians 5:25

A Magic Pen

I wish I had a magic pen," Mark announced as he put his homework in his backpack.

"What kind of magic pen?" I asked.

"All I would have to do is put a dot on the paper and the pen would do all the work," he explained.

Mark constantly creates ways to get out of doing what needs to be done. I figured it wouldn't do any good to explain that it is the process of doing the homework that is good for him. So I just enjoyed the creative energies Mark put into his invention.

"I would turn my work in, and Miss Jett would say, 'You're done already?' " he dreamed aloud.

I smiled, remembering how I wished for the same thing when I was his age. In some respects I am still wishing for the same thing. I want to reach the end result without enduring the process of getting there.

I often try to use prayer as my magic pen, asking God to remove some undesirable circumstance from my life. If He doesn't, I pray again, more diligently, and still it may not go away. Then I pray for patience to help me handle the problem, and expect to be blessed instantly with patience. That doesn't happen either.

Prayer is not a magic pen that allows me to skip over the difficult times and jump right to the benefits. Like homework, I have to go through the difficulty to grow and learn. Character traits such as patience come from working through problems over time and learning to turn things over to God.

Prayer is actually much better than a magic pen. God knows which things are good for me and which are not. He may not answer my requests in the way I want, but His answers are always for my good.

Dear God,

Thank You for the situations that cause me to struggle. It is in these struggles that I see again Your love for me. Send Your Holy Spirit to point me to You as the source of my strength, even as You are the source of my salvation. Thank You for the privilege of sharing my life with You in prayer. In Jesus' name. Amen.

Consider it pure joy, my brothers,
whenever you face trials of many kinds,
because you know that the testing of your faith
develops perseverance. Perseverance must finish
its work so that you may be mature and complete,
not lacking anything. James 1:2–4

An Ordinary Dinner

The boys raced to my parents' front door to be the first to ring the doorbell. Angela toddled after them as Steve and I gathered the diaper bag, dinner rolls, and miscellaneous borrowed items that needed to be returned. We were still in the driveway when my dad opened the door and the boys disappeared inside the house. I could see the big smile on Dad's face as Angela said "Bam-pa!" on her way through the door.

By the time Steve and I entered the house, the boys were in the kitchen telling Grandma all about their day and Angela was trying to charm some candy out of Grandpa. Grandpa was pretending he didn't understand what "can-ny" meant, but we all knew it was only a matter of time before Angela would soften Grandpa's resolve.

With the table already set, complete with a new blue-checked tablecloth, everything seemed to be in order. But despite appearances, this was no ordinary dinner. I knew it had occurred at a great price. Besides getting dressed, cooking dinner was probably the only thing Mom had done today. And because she had made dinner, she probably would be in bed for the next day or two.

Mom has post-polio syndrome, a painful condition that greatly limits her activities. It always has delighted her to make goodies and prepare meals for her family. Now, she must carefully choose her activities.

A home-cooked dinner was a treat. But knowing Mom's sacrifice to make our meal turned an ordinary dinner into a gift of love.

Her willing sacrifice demonstrated the depth of her love for us. God also made a sacrifice. He sacrificed nothing less than His own Son. He gave up His Son so my sins would be forgiven. Because of Jesus' death and resurrection, I am righteous before God and have the promise of eternal life in heaven. The depth of God's love is clearly evident in the sacrifice He made for me.

Dear Lord,

I can't even begin to fathom the love You have for me. Help me to love others as You have loved me. In Jesus' name. Amen.

This is how God showed His love among us:
He sent His one and only Son into the world that
we might live through Him. This is love: not that
we loved God, but that He loved us and sent His
Son as an atoning sacrifice for our sins.
1 John 4:9–10

Just as I Am

"Grandpa hardly gets out of bed anymore," Steve's mom told me as we prepared to visit his grandparents the next day.

"Is he that sick?" I felt a little uneasy.

"No. It's his mind. Ever since he retired, he has felt like he doesn't have any purpose, " she explained.

Grandpa spent more than 50 years in the ministry. After he retired from being a full-time pastor, he continued working part-time in another church. Now, he had retired from that as well. This man, who had touched countless lives and spent his career serving God, lay in a rented hospital bed—viewing his work, his ministry, and his life as all but over.

After visiting first with Grandpa and then with Grandma, I looked in on Grandpa again. He was propped up in his bed talking to Steve. As I walked through the doorway to leave the room, I heard Grandpa ask Steve about my mom. Surprised, I lingered by the door. I don't usually eavesdrop, but my curiosity got the better of me. All I could hear was Grandpa's closing comment: "I will keep praying for her."

A wave of emotion rose within me. He felt worthless because he was not preaching and reaching people in his familiar capacity, yet he was still serving others in a different manner. That ministry just took on a different appearance. The fact that he was praying for my mother's well-being was no small matter to me. It encouraged me and gave me hope. He was limited by the confines of his aging body, but he was open to doing God's will.

I could see Grandpa's attitude reflected in my own life. While Grandpa felt limited by his body, I feel limited by time. I have trouble keeping up with the demands of my three children. Just the thought of getting involved on a church board, teaching Sunday school, or ringing hand bells is completely overwhelming. But God will use me right where I am. Grandpa helped me realize that God was using me. Some of those ways have been in baby-sitting, sharing our dinner, or visiting with a friend while our children play together. These don't seem like big things, but if they meet a need or encourage one of God's children, then I am serving Him right where I am.

Dear Lord,

Use me as You need me, even as You used fishermen, dressmakers, shepherds, and even children to accomplish Your kingdom work. Send Your Holy Spirit to keep me open to the opportunities for service that You place before me. In Jesus' name. Amen.

*May the God of peace, ... equip you with every-
thing good for doing His will, and may He work
in us what is pleasing to Him, through Jesus
Christ, to whom be glory for ever and ever. Amen.
Hebrews 13:20–21*

Sweaty Palms

What am I doing here? I wondered as I put the headphones on and adjusted them. I looked around the radio station studio. I must have lost my mind.

There wasn't much in the small room. A large clock on the wall indicated the show would begin in less than 10 minutes. There were three chairs around a table with three huge microphones growing out of the table's surface. One microphone was positioned in front of my face.

My heart pounded twice as fast as it should. I kneaded the palms of my hands and couldn't believe how sweaty they had become. I folded them in my lap, hoping no one would want to shake my hand.

I thought back to a time long ago, when as a young student-teacher, I had been chosen to present a devotion to the school faculty. I was nervous then too, and I had confessed my fears to Steve's grandpa, a pastor who had preached thousands of sermons. He told me, "God wants to get His message across even more than you do."

Grandpa showed me that I was a tool in God's hands. He would use me as He wanted. Because He was in control, there was no telling what could be accomplished through me.

Grandpa's words gave me the courage to speak with confidence before that assembled faculty. And over the years when I had to speak in front of a group, I would remember that God was there beside me and would give me the words that I needed, when I needed them.

As I sat in the radio station with my sweaty palms pressed together and the clock ticking the seconds away, I prayed. "God, please be with me today. Let me say the words that You would have me say. Let Your message of salvation through Jesus be shared through me." I breathed a little more freely as I finished the prayer.

After the interview was over, more than one friend told me that the message brought tears. God is able to use us to touch others with the Good News of His love for us in Christ. What a privilege.

Dear God,

Give me the confidence to do the things that You ask of me. Send Your Holy Spirit to make me strong and courageous and to assure me of Your presence and salvation. Help me to witness to my Savior, Jesus. In His name. Amen.

Commit your way to the LORD; trust in Him and He will do this: He will make your righteousness shine like the dawn, the justice of your cause like the noonday sun. Psalm 37:5-6

Climbing to the Top

Mark sat in front of the computer, totally engrossed in his game. I folded laundry nearby and glanced at the screen once in a while to check his progress.

"Yeah!" Mark said. He turned to look at me and to celebrate his victory. "I made it to the top of the mountain."

"Now what happens?" I asked. Before he could answer, the animated person on the screen caught hold of a parachute and floated all the way back down to the bottom of the mountain.

"I climb it again," Mark said and turned back to the game to check on his status.

The computer screen read: "Congratulations! You have six points. You only need 494 more points to save the mountain."

I shook my head and went back to matching socks while Mark worked math problems to earn enough money, tools, and other prizes to climb his way back up the mountain.

It seemed discouraging to me. After so much time and work, he was told he needed to "win" about 95 more times before achieving the final victory.

My spiritual life is similar to that game. It feels as though I scrape and claw to achieve some small victory. Then, before I know it, I float to the bottom of the mountain, only to begin the climb again. No matter how fast or how many times I climb, I am never able to save myself.

Praise God that I don't have to save myself. Jesus already has done that for me. God knew that I couldn't climb to heaven myself, so because of His great love for me, He provided the way for me to be saved—Jesus. Through Jesus' death and resurrection, I have forgiveness for my sins and the promise of life eternal. Although all my earthly successes amount to nothing, through Jesus' saving work, I will rise up to the greatest heights to live with Him forever.

Dear Father,

I can't make it to heaven on my own. I can try and try and try, but still I fall short. Thank You for sending Jesus to save me. Thank You for the gift of faith in Him. In Jesus' name I pray. Amen.

This righteousness from God comes through faith in Jesus Christ to all who believe. There is no difference, for all have sinned and fall short of the glory of God, and are justified freely by His grace through the redemption that came by Christ Jesus.
Romans 3:22–24

"Take It Back"

T ake it back!" My heart wants to scream at God like a child who didn't get her way. Instead my heart whimpers, "I don't understand."

I do not mean to be disrespectful, but some things test me. Sometimes I question God. Some episodes in my life shake my faith.

Amanda was 6 years old. She hadn't fully grown out of her chubby cheeks when a reckless driver stole her life. I wonder why something so terrible happened to someone so young? My head supplies the memorized passage that God is good. It recalls Romans 8:28: "And we know that in all things God works for the good of those who love Him." But it is hard for me to see the good.

I want to believe that God is good. I want to believe that God is at work, even in situations that seem senseless. I want to trust that the God who saved me from sin, death, and the devil through the death and resurrection of Jesus is also able to work in all things for good.

It is at times like this when I ask God to sustain and strengthen my faith. I identify with the father of the possessed boy. When Jesus questioned him about his faith, he responded, "I do believe; help me overcome my unbelief!" (Mark 9:24). I hear myself saying those words. And I know that God hears my prayer and does send His Holy Spirit to strengthen my faith.

Dear Lord,

I don't understand everything that happens in this world. There are times when I doubt. Send Your Holy Spirit to strengthen my faith and move me past the doubt into the blessed assurance of Your love and care. For Jesus' sake. Amen.

Now we see but a poor reflection as in a mirror;
then we shall see face to face. Now I know in part;
then I shall know fully, even as I am fully known.
1 Corinthians 13:12

I Didn't Get My Way

After getting Angela and Steve settled in the hospital playroom, I marched back to the nurses' station and found Angela's nurse.

"Is the IV team going to be here soon?" I asked for what seemed like the hundredth time.

"Angela is really hungry. We need to get those tests done so she can eat. A 2-year-old can't go this long without eating."

Letty's never-ending smile didn't dim. "We finally talked to them, and they are supposed to be here soon, but we haven't seen them yet," she said.

"Okay," I said with a sigh, feeling frustrated. Everything seemed to be going wrong this morning.

I walked away from the nurses' station praying. "I don't really want Angela to be poked again. She's been poked so many times in the last two years. There are so many tests for today, and they are not going to do anything until that IV is started. And they won't let her eat until a few of those tests are done. God, please help everything to go smoothly."

I had been praying all morning, asking God to take care of this situation. I had prayed that everything would be ready as soon as we talked to the doctors. But when Angela's doctor and the head of rheumatology arrived, she still didn't have the IV. After reviewing the records and examining Angela, the rheumatologist said, "I think your daughter has Mediterranean Fever. The best way to find out is to give her the medicine and see how she responds."

"What about all the tests she's scheduled for today?"
I asked, bouncing Angela on my lap.

The doctor scanned his list. "We can always do these
tests later if the medicine doesn't work. I can give her
a prescription and send her home now," he said.

A tremendous sense of relief flooded over me. It also
became clear that God had been watching over us, even
though I hadn't felt as though things were going well. I
realized that just because I hadn't seen immediate results
to my prayers, it didn't mean God wasn't listening or
answering. God was working on the problem in a different way, just as He has many times before. For example,
instead of preventing His friend's death, Christ raised
Lazarus from the dead so those present could see God's
glory. Instead of escaping when He was arrested in the
garden, Christ endured and defeated death so we can live
with Him forever. God is truly in control of all things, and
He sends His Holy Spirit to increase our trust in Him.

Almighty God,

Help me to trust You even when things seem
to be going wrong. Answer my prayers according
to Your will and point me to the cross of Christ
when I doubt that You know what is best for me.
In Jesus' name. Amen.

*Trust in the LORD with all your heart and lean not on
your own understanding; in all your ways acknowledge Him, and He will make your paths straight.*
Proverbs 3:5–6

A Special Lesson

ngela sat on my lap while Mark and Nicholas snuggled close on either side. They all listened quietly as I read a book about a turtle. A mound of books the three children had selected was piled next to Mark. I knew that I would be reading right until bedtime.

Reading is only one pastime we enjoy. Sometimes we play games. My children excel at them. If I don't keep my head in the game, Mark will take all my checkers before I can get one king. When we can squeeze in the time, we take fun, educational family excursions. We might go to the tide pools, for a bike ride, or to the mountains to pick apples and press our own cider. I love seeing my children grow and develop.

Steve and I consider ourselves to be conscientious parents. As professional teachers, we have seen firsthand the benefits of reading, playing games, and experiencing life with our children. We make every attempt to provide positive learning experiences for them. Recently, we realized that in our effort to foster their educational growth, we had let their spiritual development slip. We had started to rely too heavily on Sunday school to provide everything they needed. We needed to support what they learned in worship services and Sunday school with devotional time at home.

I want my children to be successful in earthly pursuits, but I want much more than that. Matthew 16:26 says: "What good will it be for a man if he gains the whole world, yet forfeits his soul? Or what can a man give in exchange for his soul?" Earthly success comes to an end at death. I want my children to live forever in glory with God. That is something that all the successes in the world can't do for them. The only way to heaven is through faith in Jesus as Lord and Savior. This faith was given to them at their baptisms and is strengthened each time they encounter God in His Word. They hear this Word in worship, in Sunday school, and in our family times together. For Steve and me, teaching our children about their Savior is our most important job as parents.

Dear Lord,

Please be with me and my husband as we teach our children about You. Show us ways to instruct them and open their eyes to Your many gifts, especially the gift of Jesus, their Savior. Keep each of my children in Your loving care. Send Your Holy Spirit to guide them as they grow in their relationship with You. In Jesus' name. Amen.

Train a child in the way he should go, and when he is old he will not turn from it. Proverbs 22:6

The Potter

While on vacation, we visited an historic fort where artisans demonstrated period trades and crafts. We watched as a blacksmith heated and hammered a piece of metal. He shaped it until it became the blade of a knife. One woman was using a spinning wheel to spin thread from wool, and another was dipping candles. Everything fascinated me, but my favorite craftsman was the potter.

I watched as he took a lump of clay, smacked it down on the wheel, and started spinning it. With his hands, he formed the clay as it spun, pressing gently but firmly in one place or another to trim off excess and bring the clay into shape. "What is this going to be?" I asked as the pot seemed to grow taller.

"I'm making a pitcher," he said, talking with us while he worked.

We stayed in his workshop quite awhile, watching the pitcher being formed and chatting with the potter about his craft. Then I noticed that the pot seemed to be slightly off-center and seemed to be wobbling unevenly on the wheel. "How often do you have to start over with the clay?" I asked.

The potter pressed the sides of the pitcher in on top of itself and said, "Quite a bit today." He removed the clay from the wheel, set it aside, took a fresh lump of clay, and started spinning again. There had been no indication that there was anything wrong with his creation until it started spinning lopsidedly. It was probably only slightly off-center, but when the pitcher was big enough, the "slight bit" was enough to ruin the whole piece.

As I watched the potter work with this new clay, I thought of the references in the Bible to God as the Potter. I am like that lump of clay. God molds me with His hands and makes me into what He desires. To be shaped into the beautiful creation that God has in mind, He centers me in Jesus' saving work through the gift of faith. Then with a gentle touch here and a slight indentation there, I will spin into the vessel of God's design.

Dear Father,

Keep me focused on Jesus, the author and perfecter of my faith, as You mold me into the vessel of Your choice. Use me to spread the Good News of salvation in Jesus to all whom I meet. In Jesus' name. Amen.

Yet, O LORD, You are our Father.
We are the clay, You are the potter;
we are all the work of Your hand.
Isaiah 64:8

Shoot Me

My 13-year-old nephew, Trevor, could hardly contain his excitement. He had finally received the last piece he thought necessary for his paintball outfit—the helmet. He was itching to try the equipment.

"Don't you think you need a chest protector?" Grandpa asked Trevor at dinner.

"No, as long as I have the helmet, I will be all right," Trevor stated. Of course, a chest protector would cost more money and Trevor was out of money. He didn't want to wait until he earned the money for the additional piece.

"Luke, come outside with me. I want you to shoot me," Trevor called to his younger brother.

Luke was almost as excited as Trevor. With grins on both of their faces, they started out the door. Luke stayed on the porch with the paintball gun while Trevor ran down the hill. "Okay, Luke, shoot me!" he yelled.

Luke took careful aim and a splatter of yellow paint decorated Trevor's previously green sweats right in the middle of his chest. Trevor started back up the hill. Although the smile was still evident, it had dimmed significantly from the time he had started down the hill.

When he arrived at the house, he lifted his shirt to reveal the red, paintball-sized mark on his skin. "I think I need a chest protector," he said, moaning through his smile. The bruise still marked his chest when we left his house nearly a week later.

It would be easy to chalk up Trevor's resistance to advice as preadolescent immaturity. However, even as an adult, I do the same thing. Sometimes I get so excited about what I want to do that I refuse to listen to advice. In fact, I won't even talk to God about my desires just in case He might respond in a manner I don't want to hear. I march on with my plan until reality hits me full force. Like Trevor, it takes me a while to recover from the experience of attempting to do things on my own.

But God doesn't provide guidance that will set us back or prevent us from achieving all He has planned for us. In fact, He does just the opposite. He gives us all the facts in His Word, including the reality of our sin, the separation from Him that sin causes, our need for a Savior, the reality of the Savior He provided that first Christmas night, and the blessing of faith in Jesus through the work of the Holy Spirit.

Dear Father,

Thank You for the glorious plan of salvation You reveal to me in Your Holy Word. Help me to trust You when You tell me You have a plan for me. Remind me again and again that You are walking with me in this life, guiding me, directing me, forgiving me, and loving me. In Jesus' name. Amen.

The fear of the LORD is the beginning of wisdom; all who follow His precepts have good understanding. To Him belongs eternal praise. Psalm 111:10

Dream Castle

It was time to start Angela's cake for her third birthday party, but the cookbook wasn't on the shelf where it belonged. I remembered that Angela had been looking at the picture of her castle cake before we had left for vacation. But I couldn't recall where she might have taken the book.

Why was I so concerned about locating the missing cookbook? When anyone asked Angela what kind of party she was having, she would answer, "A p'incess potty wif a castle cake." The only thing that she was counting on for her birthday was that cake, and I couldn't find the cookbook. I had to find that recipe.

I looked everywhere. I even called my friend who had taken care of the house and pets while we were on vacation. Finally, in desperation, I called the publisher of the book. I didn't know what the publisher could do—and it was too late for them to send me a new copy—but it was my last hope.

"Yes, I know exactly which book you are talking about," the customer service representative said. "We don't print that one anymore."

"Oh, you don't," I said, feeling defeated. I tried to construct the cake from memory.

"I think we have an old copy on the shelf. If we do, I can fax it to you. Do you have a fax number?"

"My dad has one at work," I answered, trying to keep my excitement in check.

I hung up the phone so she could look for the book. While she searched her shelves, I called my dad to get his fax number. Before the day was over, she had found the book, faxed the recipe to my dad, and I had started baking Angela's castle cake.

This desperation phone call reminded me of my prayer life. Often I exhaust all my options before turning to God for help. Only in desperation do I finally call on my heavenly Father. The solutions He identifies may be things I never had considered. But I can turn to God first rather than last, trusting in His gracious love for me that wants only the best for His precious child.

Dear Lord,

Remind me that I don't have to exhaust all my options before turning to You. You love me so much that You offered Your Son as a sacrifice on the cross to win me back from sin, death, and the devil. As my loving Father, You stand always ready to help. In my Savior's name. Amen.

"Ask and it will be given to you;
seek and you will find; knock
and the door will be opened to you.
For everyone who asks receives;
he who seeks finds; and to him who knocks,
the door will be opened." Matthew 7:7–8

I Want More!

I poured just enough cereal into Angela's bowl to cover the bottom of the dish. As I set the box down and picked up the milk, Angela cried, "I wan' more!"

"I will give you more. But you need to eat this first," I explained. Continually tossing out fingered but uneaten food left on plates had taught me to offer small helpings and allow seconds and thirds instead.

"No! I wan' more now!" Angela demanded.

I poured milk into her bowl. "You can have as much as you want, but I don't want to throw cereal away. Eat this, then I will give you more."

"Nooooooo!" She started to cry, as 2-year-olds are known to do.

I sat next to her at the table and ate my cereal while she cried. She refused to take even a single bite.

As I munched my breakfast, I thought about how I sometimes act like Angela. I am consumed by a desire for more when I don't even use, or enjoy, what I have. If I use all my resources and need more, God will provide what I need just as easily as I could refill Angela's bowl.

In Matthew 25, the servants who made use of what the master gave them were praised by their master and were put in charge of even more. But one servant did not use what he was given, and he lost what little he had. As I use what God has given me, whether it is talents, money, or other blessings, I can trust Him to satisfy my needs through His gracious love. I trust Him because He kept His promise to send a Savior—a promise He made to Adam and Eve and repeated throughout history until it was fulfilled in Jesus Christ. God has given me enough for now. And if I need more, He will give me that too.

Dear Lord,

Thank You for all that You have given me, including my faith in Jesus Christ. Help me to take even the smallest blessings and use them to the fullest. In Your Son's name. Amen.

Consider the ravens: They do not sow or reap,
they have no storeroom or barn;
yet God feeds them. And how much
more valuable you are than birds!
Luke 12:24

The Right Present

Steve's mom had just started cutting onions for the next layer of the casserole when she heard the cat scratching at the back door. Still holding the knife, Lynda hurried to the door to let Zipper in the house. As soon as the door opened, Zipper picked up a dead bird, hurried inside, and dropped the animal at Lynda's feet. Lynda jumped back and a scream escaped her lips. Zipper sat down by his treasure and looked at Lynda. The tip of his tail switched back and forth as he took pride in his gift.

"Steeeee-ven!" Lynda yelled. "Come get this thing out of here!"

Zipper was showing Lynda his love for her by bringing her a gift. The only problem was that it was not the kind of gift Lynda wanted or needed.

The trick to giving a good gift is giving something that will be of value to the recipient. When my mom arrived home after a brief hospital stay, my brother and I brought her flowers. But my dad gave her the best gift. He stopped at the store on his way home from work and picked up a head of lettuce. Because lettuce had been so expensive recently, Mom had been going without salads. Dad knew how much she had been hungering for a salad and thought the greens would cheer her up more than roses. They did.

God knows what I hunger for. He knows what I need and what will bring me joy. He continually gives me good things. He gave me the greatest gift possible when He gave me eternal life. Jesus died on the cross to pay for my sins and rose again on Easter morning so I could receive eternal life in heaven. What more could I ask for? Yet God is still there, showering me with blessings and showing me His incredible love.

Dear Father,

You have given me such tremendous gifts—gifts greater than I deserve and far more wonderful than I expect. Thank You for Your perfect love in Jesus, my Savior. In His name. Amen.

"Which of you, if his son asks for bread,
will give him a stone? Or if he asks for a fish,
will give him a snake? If you, then, though
you are evil, know how to give good gifts to your
children, how much more will your Father
in heaven give good gifts to those who ask Him!"
Matthew 7:9–11

Lost and Found

But I returned all 13 books I had on Thursday. I counted them five times," I argued with the librarian on the other end of the phone.

"Our records show that *Morris and Boris at the Circus* is overdue," the woman said. The librarian continued by reading aloud all the information on her computer screen. She knew when I had checked out the book and that it had already been renewed once. She told me it couldn't be renewed again. She even looked on the shelf to make sure it hadn't been returned without being recorded.

After hanging up the phone, I checked my receipt. I had taken out 14 books, not 13, and *Morris and Boris at the Circus* was one of them.

"Okay, everyone, who knows where *Morris and Boris at the Circus* is?" I asked my family.

No one knew.

"We have to find it so we can take it back to the library. The librarian said it is green," I announced.

Our Saturday morning activities came to a screeching halt as everyone scoured the house for the lost book. We looked under couches, in toy boxes, and even in the garage. Finally, Steve found it in a pile of things under the desk in the boys' room.

Relief spread over me as I announced to the rest of the family, "We found it!"

I felt like the woman in the Bible who lost a coin, so she cleaned and searched her house until she found it. Then when she found the coin, she called her friends to come and rejoice with her. Jesus told this parable to illustrate how God searches for His lost children. Then, when even one is saved, it is cause for celebration.

I was relieved when I found the library book. The woman in the Bible rejoiced when she found her coin. But when one of God's lost children is saved, the joy is unrivaled. I can only imagine the magnificent party that takes place in heaven when one of God's children is found. Every time God gives me the opportunity to reach out to someone who is lost with the wonderful message of Jesus' saving work on the cross, I, too, can rejoice that I am included in the celebration.

Dear heavenly Father,

Show me those who are lost and in need of hearing the message of Jesus' death and resurrection on our behalf. Use me to accomplish Your purposes here on earth and to proclaim Your gracious love to all I meet. In Jesus' name. Amen.

*"In the same way, I tell you, there is rejoicing
in the presence of the angels of God
over one sinner who repents."
Luke 15:10*

Pretty Good
for Someone Who Doesn't Sew

I finished sewing a seam and turned toward Steve. As I held up part of the quilt top, I asked, "How does it look?"

Steve admired my handiwork, "That's turning out nicely." Then he added, "It's pretty good, for someone who doesn't sew."

I grinned and turned back to the sewing machine. As I lined up the next piece to add to the quilt, I thought, *God must laugh when He hears me say I can't or won't do something.* Perhaps God enjoys showing me that even if I can't, He can.

I was telling everyone I knew that I didn't sew. I was proud of the fact. Then God introduced me to Susie, who loves to sew. In fact, her favorite pastime is making quilts. I thought she was a strange bird, but since she had other qualities I admired, I knew we would be friends.

When Susie turned her passion for sewing into an opportunity to serve others, she wanted me to join her. At first I was hesitant, but slowly she convinced me—a self-proclaimed non-seamstress—to give it a try for God.

Not only did I begin to sew a baby quilt and to pray for an unidentified child, but God showed me that He could use me in ways I would never have thought possible. He began to shape me into a person He could use to accomplish His purposes here on earth, whether or not I thought I had the necessary gifts. He showed me that "I will never" or "I can't" have no place in a believer's vocabulary because with Him, we can accomplish anything.

Dear God,

You are amazing. You accomplish so much through me, a poor sinful human being. Thank You for the forgiveness that is mine through Jesus for the times I misuse Your gifts to me. Forgive me for those times I walk away instead of following Your call to serve others. Help me to live my life in daily service to You as I share Your love with those around me. In Jesus' name. Amen.

I can do everything through Him
who gives me strength.
Philippians 4:13

Piecing a Quilt

I ran my hand over the fabric folded on the table in front of me. The brightly colored fish contrasted with the stark black background. This would be the primary fabric for the quilt I was going to make. I also had bright yellow material and, for the backing, a green-checked piece. These designs would make a fun quilt, especially for a little boy.

The quilting teachers handed each student a folder with the directions. The first step was to cut the yellow cloth and the fish cloth into pieces. This was all I accomplished in the first class. During the next class, I sewed some of the pieces together, then cut them again. This cutting and sewing continued, according to the plan, until I had the quilt top completed.

As I examined my handiwork, I thought, *I started with a big piece of fabric. Now after about 10 hours of work and a lot of cutting and sewing, I am back to one piece of fabric.*

Although it was the truth, it was a cynical point of view. I *had* come full circle, but the completed piece I held in my hands had gained character and purpose. Fish were swimming everywhere with yellow blocks adding color to the pattern.

I began to see similarities between the quilting process and the process that my heavenly Father uses to bring "wholeness" to my life. Sin tears me into little bits and pieces. But God, working through His Word and sacraments, carefully puts the pieces back together, adding bits of color here and there. Because sin is part of this world, this cutting and piecing happens over and over in my life—and it can be painful. But one day my heavenly Father will gather me and all believers together and piece us together in heaven with Jesus.

Dear Lord,

Please forgive my sins that tear me apart and seek to tear me away from You. Thank You for joining me back together and to You through the saving blood of Jesus. As I move through the trials of this life, work in me to reflect the pattern of Your love to those around me. In Jesus' name. Amen.

Not only so, but we also rejoice in our sufferings, because we know that suffering produces perseverance; perseverance, character; and character, hope. And hope does not disappoint us, because God has poured out His love into our hearts by the Holy Spirit, whom He has given us. Romans 5:3-4

Distractions

The phone rang just as I sat down to talk with Mark and Nicholas about school. My first inclination was to answer it. But with an arm around each boy and anticipating an important conversation about math tests, I ignored it. "Is anyone else on nines?" I asked Mark.

Another ring echoed through the house. "The phone is ringing," Mark said.

"I know. I'm going to let the machine get it," I answered, not moving from my spot. This time was precious to me. It was a small thing, but I hoped the boys would realize how valuable they are to me if I put them first in this small way.

More important than the precious time I have with my family is the time I have with God. But that time is often riddled with distractions, including my children. Everything may be quiet, but as soon as I begin to read my Bible or pray, one of them appears at my side to show me a picture or to ask a question. I can't ignore my children like I do the phone, but I struggle to find uninterrupted time with God.

A friend told me of a woman who had a daily "timeout for mommy." This was her time to be with God. She would take care of all the drinks and potty times, involve the children in a quiet activity, and retreat for her timeout. Another friend has a prayer chair. When she wants to pray, she sits in that chair and the children know not to disturb her.

It may take time and work to train the children not to disturb me, but if I could implement a method like one of these, I could preserve time to spend with God. In so doing, I show my children how valuable my relationship with God is.

Dear Lord,

I desire and need time with You. So often there are distractions interrupting me. Please show me how to make the time for You and tune out the other distractions. In Jesus' name. Amen.

Then Jesus went with His disciples to a place
called Gethsemane, and He said to them,
"Sit here while I go over there and pray."
Matthew 26:36

Knowing the Rules

Nicholas and Angela were finishing their lunch while I cleaned up the kitchen. "Angela, let's play rock, scissors, paper," Nicholas said and turned at the table to face his sister.

He pounded his fist in his hand, chanting "rock, scissors, paper" with each strike. Angela joined in, mimicking her brother.

"I won!" he announced. "Let's play again." And the pounding continued with Nicholas declaring victory periodically.

Then Angela joined in, "I won!"

"No, you didn't," Nicholas argued. "You had rock, and I had paper. Paper covers rock. See?" He placed his open hand over Angela's fist.

Angela smiled, and they started their hammering again. Angela kept asserting victory and Nicholas kept correcting her, but he never told her the rules of the game or even taught her how to play. She was just pounding her fist into her hand. That was enough for her. When Nicholas started saying he won, she wanted to win too. But to win, she would need to know the goal and the rules of the game.

One reason that God established His Law in Moses' time was to show the people where they stood in relation to Him. When I look at that Law, I know what the rules are and I know that I have lost. I don't meet the goal.

All is not lost for me, though. Jesus fulfilled the Law completely in my place. And He secured victory for me by sacrificing His life on the cross for me. Now, I can declare confidently, "I win!" because His resurrection shows He won forgiveness and eternal life for me.

Dear Lord,

I can't win by myself. Thank You for giving me Jesus to obtain the victory for me. In His name. Amen.

He was delivered over to death for our sins
and was raised to life for our justification.
Romans 4:25

Filling the Void

Facing the phone table, I had to shut my eyes. My task for the afternoon was to clean off this table. I dreaded this job. The table was the catchall.

As I weeded through junk, I felt like an archaeologist sifting through layers of sediment. I could estimate the dates of some of these layers by discovering party invitations or by looking at coupon expiration dates.

After the children went to bed, I finally was able to wipe down the surface that had been hidden under the piles of stuff. It felt good to have cleared all the junk away.

As I stood back to admire my work, I thought how nice it would be if it would stay clean and tidy. But I knew it wouldn't. The first time I needed to put something somewhere, it would land on this table.

Then I decided that, instead of leaving it empty and open to anything, I would deliberately put something on that table. Gathering a few things from here and there, I designed an attractive, autumn arrangement to fill the empty space. Now I knew it would be much harder to toss the junk mail there.

There are similarities between my spiritual life and my phone table. I get bogged down with garbage that messes up my life. I can clean up my act and get rid of the vices that are troubling me, but if God does not fill that empty space, evil will continue to haunt me.

Jesus explained this in Luke 11: "When an evil spirit comes out of a man, it goes through arid places seeking rest and does not find it. Then it says, 'I will return to the house I left.' When it arrives, it finds the house swept clean and put in order. Then it goes and takes seven other spirits more wicked than itself, and they go in and live there. And the final condition of that man is worse than the first."

Daily I ask God to protect me from all harm and danger and to help me act as a temple of the Most High God. Through the gift of the Holy Spirit, I am filled with God and evil can't find a home in my heart.

Dear God,

Fill me with Your Holy Spirit so there is no room for anything ugly in my life. Thank You for forgiving me for Jesus' sake for the times my life becomes cluttered with the things of this world. In Jesus' name. Amen.

May the God of hope fill you with all joy and peace as you trust in Him, so that you may over-flow with hope by the power of the Holy Spirit.
Romans 15:13

Little Red Cowboy

Nicholas walked into the living room with his new cowboy costume on and a big grin on his face.

"How does it fit?" I asked him.

"Pretty good." He looked down to examine his red, suede-looking vest and chaps.

"Turn around," I said.

He turned in a circle so I could see the back of the costume too. When he came to a stop, he stood with his feet spread to about shoulder width.

"Hey, the way you're standing with your feet apart like that looks great," I said. "You look like you have been riding a horse all day. If you stand like that for the costume contest at the Harvest Party tomorrow, you will have a better chance of winning."

His grin grew even wider.

The next day, Nicholas bounced up and down before the costume judging. But when the contest started, he stood with his feet spread and did his best to look like a real cowboy.

After several prizes had been given away to cute little babies and toddlers, my 6-year-old inched his feet out a little farther. A few more prizes were awarded. He widened his stance even more. Finally, the judges announced, "The last prize is for the best boy costume."

Nicholas slid his feet apart as far as they would go. Now instead of looking like he had ridden a horse, he looked like he had been on an elephant.

Please, choose Nicholas, I thought. *He wants to win so much.*

"The winner is ..." I held my breath. "Daniel Boone."

I hugged my sad little cowboy; he had tried so hard.

I thought about how sometimes I try my best, and no matter how hard I try, I don't succeed in winning the prize or attaining my goal. I may stretch as far as I can, but instead of getting closer, I look like I've been riding an elephant.

I am woefully imperfect in God's eyes—without Jesus. But with Jesus, I am the best. It's sort of like wearing a costume. Through Baptism, I have put on Christ. Now God sees Christ's righteousness, not my imperfections. When I die, I know I will win the prize and be with my Lord forever in heaven.

Dear Lord,

When I am trying to do everything on my own, focus me on the cross and the reality of Jesus' sacrifice for me. Thank You for my robe of righteousness. Keep me safe in Your care until we meet face-to-face. In Jesus' name. Amen.

Therefore, if anyone is in Christ,
he is a new creation; the old has gone,
the new has come! 2 Corinthians 5:17

Work, Work, Work

"Mark, I need you to put away your clothes," I called as I finished folding and hanging up three loads of laundry.

Mark stomped into my bedroom. "All you want me to do is work, work, work. I never get any time to play!"

I stared at him without saying a word. After I had spent what seemed like an entire afternoon sorting, folding, and hanging up laundry, he had the nerve to complain about the simplest chore. I looked at my bed, which was covered with piles of neatly folded underwear, socks, shorts, and T-shirts. "Sweetheart," I said slowly, "I folded all of this. You can put your own things away."

It took Mark a couple of minutes to carry his stacks to his room. I thought of all I do for my son—wash his clothes, feed him, clean his house, and purchase all the things he needs. I also spend time reading with him, going to his classroom, and teaching his Sunday school class. It's hard to believe that he could complain about doing a simple task I give to him.

I wonder if God sometimes feels as dismayed with me as I was with Mark. He has given me absolutely everything I have. He created me, provides for all my needs, even sacrificed His own Son so I could have forgiveness and life everlasting. Then when He asks a little something of me, I complain because it's too much.

What God asks of me is so very little in comparison to what He has given me. When I stop and look at all that

God has blessed me with, I realize that I can't do enough for Him. I can't give Him enough thanks and praise.

Dear Lord,

Thank You for all that You have given me and all that You have done for me. Without You, I would be nothing and have nothing. Help me respond to You with a grateful heart. In Jesus' name. Amen.

Your attitude should be the same as that of
Christ Jesus: who, being in very nature God,
did not consider equality with God something
to be grasped, but made Himself nothing,
taking the very nature of a servant,
being made in human likeness.
And being found in appearance as a man,
He humbled Himself and became obedient
to death—even death on a cross!
Philippians 2:5–8

Do It for Me

I dragged myself out of bed, grabbing a tissue on my way to the kitchen. "You boys need to get dressed and have your breakfast quickly so you don't miss the bus," I said.

Mark and Nicholas disappeared into their room. My head felt like it was twice its usual size as I stood at the counter making peanut butter and jelly sandwiches for their lunch. My cold was not enough to keep me in bed, but I had no energy.

Angela sat at the table. "Mommy, I'm hungry!" she announced.

Nicholas came back, whining, "Mark won't help me find my jeans."

I sighed. I was going to have to locate a pair of pants for Nicholas before I poured Angela some cereal. Mark was dressed when he came in, asking for help with his buttons. "Mark," I said, "anything you can do to help your brother or sister this morning will help me."

As soon as I said this, I thought about the Bible verse in Matthew 25:40: "The king will reply, 'I tell you the truth, whatever you did for one of the least of these brothers of Mine, you did for Me.' " I want to do things for Jesus, but I don't often think of the little things as being of much service to God. However, the small things I do for someone else are not small at all to that person.

God loves all of His children and meeting a need of one of these children is a way to serve God. Mark helped me by pouring his sister's cereal and saving me a trip to the back of the house to find Nicholas' pants. Although they did not seem important to Mark, these tasks had to be done.

The next time I become frustrated with tasks that I do for someone else, I'll remember the lesson I learned when I was sick. Then I will visualize Jesus' face, knowing that I am really serving Him.

Dear God,

Sometimes I don't feel like helping other people, especially when I have to put aside my own needs. Remind me that it is You I am serving and give me a spirit of willingness to help. In Jesus' name. Amen.

Whatever you do, work at it with all your heart,
as working for the Lord, not for men,
since you know that you will receive
an inheritance from the Lord as a reward.
It is the Lord Christ you are serving.
Colossians 3:23–24

Swinging High

"I wanna swing!" Angela yelled as she and her friend, Shannon, ran for the swings. Each one claimed her spot and climbed on a swing.

I had barely begun to push the two girls when Angela called out, "Higher! Higher!"

I gave my daughter a firm boost, and the breeze blew her blonde hair back from her face.

"Push me higher too," Shannon sang out.

I gave her a little push.

"That's enough!" she protested, a little tremor in her voice.

"Again, Mommy!" Angela called. "Again!" She had noticed my attention had turned to Shannon. Another couple shoves and she was on her way.

"I want to go higher too." Shannon joined in. "Not too much."

This continued with Angela thinking that she couldn't get enough altitude and Shannon wanting to go higher yet at the same time feeling afraid. So I pushed Angela higher and gave Shannon gentle pushes now and then.

Of the two girls, I can relate to Shannon best. I see the heights and tell God, "Take me higher. I want to go to the top." But when God starts to push me, I feel afraid and don't want to go any further. I give into the fear that I might fall.

But when I pushed Angela, I pushed her only as high as I thought safe. She wanted to go higher, but I didn't take the risk. In the same way, God does not push me harder or higher than I can go. Knowing this, I can, like Angela, ask God to take me to greater heights and trust that He knows my limits even better than I do.

Dear Father,

Take me to the heights that You want me to go. I know that You have done everything to make me Your child, including the sacrifice of Your Son, so You will always be by my side, no matter how scary it seems. In my Savior's name. Amen.

"But blessed is the man who trusts in the LORD, whose confidence is in Him. He will be like a tree planted by the water that sends out its roots by the stream. It does not fear when heat comes; its leaves are always green. It has no worries in a year of drought and never fails to bear fruit."
Jeremiah 17:7

Helpers

"Ower da wiver and tru da woods to Bam-ma's house we go." Angela sang along with her brothers in the backseat of Grandma's car. This had become one of her favorite songs.

When the children had finished singing the first verse, the boys stopped, but Angela wanted to continue. "Sing wif me, Mok and Nick," she said.

"No. You'll just mess it up," Nicholas said as he played with the toys he had brought. Mark already was engrossed in play and didn't even respond.

"No, I won't, if you hep me," Angela answered.

"Yes, you will," Nicholas said.

"I can do it if you hep me," Angela said, swinging her feet in her car seat.

"No!" Nicholas wouldn't be persuaded.

So Angela tried a solo: "It 'tings and bites the nose and toes—"

"See, I told you that you would mess it up," Nicholas interrupted.

"Because you wouldn't hep me," Angela said to defend herself.

Angela had a point. She wasn't going to learn the song if she couldn't get any help. She had mastered the first verse, now she was pushing on to the second verse. But the boys didn't want to bother teaching her another verse.

There have been times when I didn't want to be bothered with helping someone else, especially if I didn't think it would do any good. For example, I didn't feel too helpful when my brother called to ask for a ride because his car had broken down again.

But God has reached out to me with the gift of salvation. He has freed me to be His servant and to share His love with others. In grateful response to all God has done for me in Christ, I can reach out to others, even if I think the situation seems hopeless. What may be hopeless to me is quite possible to God.

God reaches out to all people and offers them a future glory through the death and resurrection of His Son. I can trust Him to provide the way for me to serve others in His name.

Dear Lord,

Help me reach out to all people with Your love. Allow me to see You work wonders in their lives, even as You have worked the wonder of salvation in my life. In Jesus' name. Amen.

May Your unfailing love rest upon us, O LORD,
even as we put our hope in You. Psalm 33:22

Boing!

I dashed into the house after a doctor's appointment. I had to arrange the turkey slices on the platter and take it to school for the boys' Thanksgiving feast.

As I was rolling the thin pieces of meat, the phone rang.

"This is Tammy from the bank," a voice said. "There are three checks waiting to clear, but there is not enough money in your account."

"Oh, dear," I said with a gasp.

"You need to bring the money to cover them by noon or we will have to return them," she explained.

"Okay, I'll be there."

I didn't have time to figure out what had gone wrong. I took the money out of savings and put it in the checking account, making a mental note to check the details after the feast.

When I sat down with the bank statement and the checkbook later, I found mistake after mistake. I had recorded one item wrong, omitted a check, and forgotten to note a fee.

After sorting out all the finances, I was in a sour mood. Those careless errors combined with the bank penalties would take all the money we had saved the last several months.

When we left for the Thanksgiving church service that evening, I did not have a very thankful attitude. But the pastor talked about taking inventory of what we have, not what we don't have, and thanking God for what He has given us.

I thought about my banking problems. I had been focusing on all the money that we no longer had. Now I was beginning to see how God had provided the solution for our money troubles. We had enough to cover the situation, which was all we needed.

In the same way, God has provided the solution for my sin debt—Jesus. He knew I didn't have the ability to cover this debt on my own, so Jesus took all my sins to the cross. My bill is stamped "Paid in Full" because of the blood my Savior shed for me. Now I have the freedom to live for Him on this earth and the promise of eternal life. That's quite a savings account!

Dear Lord,

Thank You for all Your many blessings. Thank You for providing the answer to my greatest need through the death and resurrection of Jesus. Thank You also for handling my daily needs and the needs of my family. In Jesus' name. Amen.

Therefore, since we are receiving a kingdom that cannot be shaken, let us be thankful, and so worship God acceptably with reverence and awe.
Hebrews 12:28

Giving

Mark, Nicholas, and Angela thoroughly investigated the entire toy aisle, looking for just the right Christmas gift for a needy child. They carefully selected a car carrier and two packages of automobiles. Then we moved on to the clothing department.

"We have to get this car shirt," Mark said. "It's so cool!" I looked at the basket and mentally tallied how much I was already spending.

"If we get the shirt, we might have to put back one of the packs of cars," I said.

"No!" Mark argued. "We have to have at least eight cars to fill up all the spaces on the trailer."

I sighed and gave in. I was actually pleased that he was concerned about these matters, even though the presents were going to a child we didn't know.

I placed the basket next to the register. The checker handed each child a little package. "Would you children like a card game?" she asked.

"Thank you," they each said as they received their unexpected surprise.

On the way out, I said, "Since you all got a game, maybe we could give one to the needy child. We don't need to have three of the same game."

"Not mine!" they each said in turn.

I chewed on my lip. *I guess this is where the generosity stops,* I thought. *It's fine when it comes out of Daddy's pocket, but they don't want to share from their own treasures.*

I felt frustrated with my children, but I'm not so different. I'm all for God helping other people, but at times, I don't want to be involved personally. It takes too much time or too much money. Both of those seem to be in short supply.

But God provided everything for me when He sent His only Son to suffer and die for my sins. He has provided all my earthly resources as well. I can afford to be generous because what I have actually comes from God's pockets, and His pockets are deep.

Dear Father,

Help me to be generous with the blessings You have given me to share. Especially help me to share the Good News of Jesus with those around me. In His name I pray. Amen.

Now He who supplies seed to the sower
and bread for food will also supply and
increase your store of seed and will enlarge
the harvest of your righteousness. You will be
made rich in every way so that you can be
generous on every occasion, and through us
your generosity will result in thanksgiving to God.
2 Corinthians 9:10–11

What Is in a Name?

I walked to the pharmacy counter to pick up antibiotics for each of the boys. Dana, the pharmacy tech, was busy with a customer, so he called to the back for someone else to help.

"Prescriptions for Duerr," I told the woman when she asked if she could help me.

As she reached for the bottles, Dana said, "The co-pay is pretty high on one of those, Cathy."

I looked at the paperwork and winced at the amount. "I also wondered why they gave Mark such a harsh antibiotic in the first place. But what can I do about it?" I asked.

"We can call the doctor and see if there is something else he could prescribe," Dana offered.

"That sounds like a good idea. Let's do that."

Dana finished helping his customer and went to make the call.

I wandered off to look through the store, thankful that Dana knew me well enough to offer to make the call. It's nice to be known and to feel that someone has my best interests at heart. Dana was able to get a milder antibiotic for Mark, which saved me money. That personal attention keeps me returning to the same pharmacy.

Dana's knowledge of me is limited to what he sees when I come in for medicine. But someone knows me even better and is always concerned about my well-being.

God knows me intimately, knows every little detail of my life. He looks out for me. Not only is He willing to call problems to my attention and fix them, He sent His only Son, who laid down His life for me.

I can rest assured that I am known and well taken care of because I am God's beloved child.

Dear Father,

You know me inside and out. I ask forgiveness for my sins for Jesus' sake and come to You for peace and rest in Your tender care. In my Savior's name. Amen.

*I am the good shepherd; I know My sheep
and My sheep know Me—just as the Father knows
Me and I know the Father—and I lay down
My life for the sheep. John 10:14–15*

Individual Needs

I tired," Angela complained as we ate our lunch.

"Do you want to take a nap?" I asked her.

"No. I not tired anymore," she said, sitting up a little straighter.

I smiled. Angela was never tired if she might have to take a nap. She had felt warm to me all morning. Then I looked at her sandwich. She had only taken one bite and was not eating anymore. Past experience told me that she was getting sick.

I looked at the clock. *If I put her down now, she won't be awake by the time I need to pick Nicholas up at school,* I thought.

Sweet Nicholas. That morning he had appeared in the kitchen with a coupon for a ride home from school. I could tell that it wasn't so much that he desired transportation, but that he needed Mommy. I rarely "promise" to pick the boys up after school; I just show up if I can. But today …

Angela needed a nap. I sighed.

"Angela, come with me. We are going to take a nap-nap." I told her, taking her by the hand. We walked to her bedroom.

"I not tired," she protested, but she came with me willingly.

As I lay next to Angela, I wondered what to do about Nicholas.

After Angela was asleep, I called my friend Jean and explained my dilemma. "Is there any way you could sit with Angela just long enough for me to get Nicholas and come back?" I asked.

When Nicholas came out of his classroom after school and saw me, his whole face lit up. I knew all the trouble had been worth it.

Just as I do my best to give my children what they need, God provides for my individual needs in an even more wonderful way. He knows when I need a nap or special one-on-one time with Him and that's exactly what He provides. And He knew my greatest need and supplied His only Son as the payment I could not make for my sins. Because of Jesus' death and resurrection, I am free to call God *Abba, Father.*

Dear Father,

Thank You for knowing all my needs and blessing me so richly. Thank You for the gift of faith in Your Son. Strengthen me for the day's tasks. In Jesus' name. Amen.

And my God will meet all your needs
according to His glorious riches in Christ Jesus.
Philippians 4:19

Level Ground

Angela and her friend Austin dumped out the bucket of cars and spread them out so they could choose which ones they wanted to drive on the mat. While the 3-year-olds played, Austin's mom and I visited and watched Addison, the baby, to keep her out of trouble. She crawled through the cars, played with the stuffed animals, and cruised along the furniture.

Crawling over to the couch, Addison pulled herself up to where her mother sat. She got the smile and reassurance she needed and was off again. She held onto the couch as she inched her way along. She came to where the big kids had dumped the cars, but she kept going.

I watched as Addison took each little step, right on top of the cars. She was unsteady on her feet as it was, so trying to keep her balance on the bumpy, unpredictable surface made it even more difficult to walk. It would have been so much easier if Addison had gone around the cars.

I noticed a similarity in my life. When I take off on my own, I usually come across obstacles that I have to climb over. But God comes to me to lead me onto level ground. When I follow God's way and do His will, the surface is smoother. On my own, I'm unsteady on my feet. But God has sent His Holy Spirit through Word and sacraments to keep me on the right path, to keep me steady. I don't have to walk alone—God walks with me.

Dear Father,

You know what is ahead for me. Lead me along the path You choose for me. When I come across obstacles, help me onto the smooth ground again. In Jesus' name. Amen.

Teach me to do Your will, for You are my God;
may Your good Spirit lead me on level ground.
Psalm 143:10

Burden

ick climbed down the steps of the school bus and emerged through the door. He smiled at me, but his hair was sweaty, his face looked drawn, and if it hadn't been for the backpack holding him erect, I'm sure his body would have sagged forward.

As he hugged me, he slid the backpack off. "Can you carry this?" he asked.

"Sure," I said, taking the strap with one hand and his little hand with the other. As we walked down the street to our house, I asked, "What's in this thing?"

"My lunch box and my reading book and my folder..."

When we got home, I opened the pack to check its contents. "Nick, why are you carrying this big heavy binder around?"

"It has my folder and my notebook in it," he answered.

Both items were empty. "This notebook is supposed to stay at school so you can put your work for math club in it. And this folder doesn't need to be in this binder. You can take these things out and you won't have to carry such a heavy load," I explained.

A few days later, I sat in church, listening to the pastor speak about giving our burdens to Jesus. I thought of Nick and his backpack. He gave me his backpack to carry for him. While I had it, I lightened the load he would lift later. He didn't need that whole burden, so we got rid of some of it.

at I carry a lot of stuff that isn't necessary.
es me to give Him my burdens. He will carry
hat is too heavy for me to bear, including my
ict, He carried that burden all the way to the
d left it there, giving me the feather-light robe of
isness instead. What a privilege to know that I
e it all to Him and He will get rid of the excess
ze that I don't need to worry about.

Dear Father.

I tend to haul things around with me that I don't
need to carry. I bring my burdens to You. Help me
to leave them with You and only to bear the things
You want me to bear. In Jesus' name. Amen.

*Come to Me, all you who are
weary and burdened,
and I will give you rest.
Matthew 11:28*

A Great Future

My friend Kelly and I sat in the stands, watching our 7-year-old boys warm up for their game. "That Drew of yours is going to play professional baseball when he grows up. Then he can take care of you in your old age," I said to tease my friend.

She laughed. I knew she didn't know what to say. Agreeing with me would seem immodest, but in truth, she couldn't deny the possibility. Drew has been playing in baseball leagues since he was 2 ½ years old. He is naturally talented. He also has parents that nurture his talent and provide numerous ways to develop his skills. I would not be at all surprised to see him playing professional baseball someday.

After the boys finished their game, Drew came over to the stands. He tried to smile, but I could tell he was disappointed that his team had lost the game. He likes to win. Although his parents are sympathetic to Drew's disappointment, they don't worry too much about wins or losses. A single loss at this level is insignificant when compared to the larger picture. Drew's parents are more interested in perfecting his skills and building him into a competent ballplayer, rather than his win/loss record.

This made me think about how I experience the difficulties and disappointments in my life. Like Drew's parents, God is sympathetic to my disappointment. His real concern, however, is my growth and development as His child and how each event in my life contributes to this process. In both the good and the bad, God sees the bigger picture. He sees the path He has planned for me as His beloved daughter. He also sees what His Holy Spirit will need to do in my life as I walk the road to my heavenly home.

I sometimes feel like God doesn't care about my pain. But He does care. He understands perfectly because His only Son, Jesus, experienced the same pain and disappointments while He lived on earth. God is always there to offer comfort and to help me continue. God is not as interested in the temporal as He is in the eternal. He can't wait until I'm in heaven with Him, and through His gift to me of faith in Jesus, He has done everything necessary to make sure I'm victorious on that final day. What tremendous love God has for me—now and forever.

Dear Lord,

Please soothe my hurts. So often I don't understand Your ways, but please send Your Holy Spirit to help me grow into the person You want me to be. In my Savior's name. Amen.

"For I know the plans I have for you," declares the LORD, *"plans to prosper you and not to harm you, plans to give you hope and a future."*
Jeremiah 29:11

Holding Hands

gave Nicholas a good-bye kiss and a big squeeze. He hurried to line up with the other kindergartners as they went into the classroom. As soon as he got in position, he turned around and gave me one last wave.

Once he was inside, I took Angela's hand in mine and we started toward the car. She bounced along beside me, talking and laughing. As we approached the parking lot, I looked to make sure no cars were coming. When I got to the curb, I didn't need to stop, the coast was clear.

Angela didn't even hesitate at the curb. She stepped off, oblivious to any possible danger, and kept going, holding onto my hand as she went. I looked at her and saw her carefree attitude. She trusted me. With her hand in mine, she followed along without worry.

Of course, she was only 2 years old. She did not fully grasp the dangers of a parking lot. She allowed me to lead her. She trusted me.

If only I could have that much trust. I want to put my hand in my Father's hand and let Him take me wherever He wants. But sometimes, when we get to the curb, I stop and check to see if it looks safe. I hesitate because it looks like a big step down into the parking lot. Or if God wants to lead me into places where I can't see, I hold back, saying, "I don't know where we are going."

This is God I am talking about. The same God who created me, offered His Son as a sacrifice to save me, and walks with me wherever I go. I know that God is always there with me. No matter where He takes me, I can go confidently, knowing I will be safe. With His hand snugly holding mine, I can go anywhere.

Dear Father,

Take me wherever You want. I know You are holding my hand and won't let me fall. In my Savior's name. Amen.

Yet I am always with You; You hold me by my right hand. You guide me with Your counsel, and afterward You will take me into glory.
Psalm 73:23–24